What Is Post-Modern Conservatism?

Essays On Our Hugely Tremendous Times

What Is Post-Modern Conservatism?

Essays On Our Hugely Tremendous Times

Edited and Assembled by

Matthew McManus

With Additional Essays by Dylan DeJong, Borna Radnik, David Hollands, Erik Tate, Conrad Bongard Hamilton

zero books

Winchester, UK
Washington, USA

JOHN HUNT PUBLISHING

First published by Zero Books, 2020
Zero Books is an imprint of John Hunt Publishing Ltd., No. 3 East St., Alresford,
Hampshire SO24 9EE, UK
office@jhpbooks.com
www.johnhuntpublishing.com
www.zero-books.net

For distributor details and how to order please visit the 'Ordering' section on our website.

ISBN: 978 1 78904 245 0
978 1 78904 246 7 (ebook)
Library of Congress Control Number: 2019905181

A CIP catalogue record for this book is available from the British Library.

Design: Stuart Davies

UK: Printed and bound by CPI Group (UK) Ltd, Croydon, CR0 4YY
US: Printed and bound by Thomson-Shore, 7300 West Joy Road, Dexter, MI 48130

Contents

Dedicated to the memory of our friend
Connor O'Callaghan

Acknowledgements

Most of the essays compiled here were published between November 2017 and July 2018 in various outlets including: *The New Politics, Quillette, Political Critique, The McGill International Review, Areo, The Hill Times, Merion West, The Australian Spectator* and *The Philosophical Salon.* They have been reprinted with permission and with the gratitude of the author for supporting his work in these strange times. They have been lightly edited to fit into this volume.

The authors would like to thank their families, friends, significant others for their support, including Professor Marion Trejo of TEC de Monterrey. Special thanks go to York University, Kingston University and especially the University of TEC de Monterrey for their financial and institutional assistance. Finally we would like to acknowledge the work of Peter Lawler, who coined the term post-modern conservatism in books such as *Post-Modernism Rightly Understood* and other works. While he was a pioneer in his analysis, we would like to acknowledge that we were made aware of Lawler's work late in this project, and that our use of the term "post-modern conservative" has little resemblance to his own. Lawler understands post-modern conservatism as a form of Thomistic realism. Our interpretation is considerably more critical. Thank you to Zero Books for supporting our work and publishing these essays. Finally, a special commemoration for our friend Connor O'Callaghan, who tragically passed away during the writing of this collection.

Preface

The Five Features of Postmodern Conservatism

Matt McManus

Introduction

The essays in this book summarize many of the main features we associate with what we call "post-modern conservatism." They operate primarily at a general level discussing broad topics in intellectual history, social theory, and current events across the globe. Before we move on to some heavier listing, this preface will present a short list of characteristics I feel one can use to identify and categorize post-modern conservatism in its most common manifestations. This may well help to concretize the main ideas for those who may be sympathetic to my arguments but are nonetheless unsure of how they can be positively applied to help us better interpret and change the world.

Before I begin I would like to offer two caveats to this position. Firstly, when characterizing post-modern conservatives, I by no means intend to imply that the category applies to all those who identify with conservatism or who hold right wing views. Conservatism is a complex outlook with a deep history, and is neither one thing nor the other. Its post-modern variant is just the latest variation to emerge, and by no means the only one. Indeed some conservative figures are staunchly opposed to the rise and emergence of post-modern conservatism and have pushed against it with a vengeance. This includes many natural law conservatives, right wing Roman Catholics, a significant number of neoliberals and so on. Secondly, the list I am presenting is neither exhaustive and does not strictly apply in all circumstances. Some of the features I list may apply more rigidly to certain post-modern conservatives, and others not at all. But when taken together they provide a relatively comprehensive overview that should be helpful when distinguishing post-modern conservatives from others. There are five features that I think are characteristic:

1. A dismissal of rational standards for interpreting facts and values
2. Appeal to a traditionally powerful identity as a source for truth and a narrative of victimization and resentment demanding its return to the top of the social hierarchy
3. A contradictory and reactionary political ideology
4. Despite being reactionaries, post-modern conservatives deploy hyper-modern media to promulgate their political ideology
5. Once in power, postmodern conservatives actively crack down on other identity groups. Uniquely, this includes those who hold other epistemic and meta-ethical standards in order to preserve the hollow integrity of the victim narrative and its consequent political ideology. This leads to the perpetuation of the post-modern culture which birthed them in the first place. It is also coupled with calls for the effacement of traditional institutional and ideological barriers to the realization of the post-modern conservative political program

I will discuss each of these briefly in turn.

1. *A Dismissal of Rational Standards for Interpreting Facts and Values*

The claim often made about post-modern conservatives, most noticeably Trump and his acolytes, is that they are prone to lying. While understandable, I think this misrepresents what is distinct about Trump's approach to the truth. As Harry Frankfurt of *On*

Bullshit fame indicated, a liar is someone who still has some tangential sense of what the truth is. They are aware of what is true and choose to dishonestly present the opposite. This is not true of Trump and his acolytes.

What characterizes a post-modern conservative is indifference to the whole dualism of truth and falsehood as traditionally understood. Many philosophers and politicians have debated for centuries about what is true and false in the world factually, and which are the true values we should uphold in our political systems. Postmodern conservatism implicitly rejects even the possibility that there could be such a thing as factual truth or objective values which can be ascertained by any objective means. Part of this stems from the association post-modern conservatives make between traditional standards and means of assessing the truth of facts and values and "elite" personalities who they regard as antagonistic to their interests. They reject such standards, and seek to put in their place those which are conducive to the traditional identity they affiliate with and the victim narrative that forms the core of the post-modern conservative political ideology. This means that anything that deviates from the values of that identity is dismissed as bias (http://merionwest.com/2018/06/21/on-bias-and-truth-in-the-public-sphere/)

2. *Appeal to a traditionally powerful identity as a source for truth and a narrative of victimization and resentment demanding its return to the top of the social hierarchy.*

Post-modern conservatives typically belong to or affiliate with social identities who have traditionally wielded most of the power in Western societies. There are many variations on this, and often the affiliation of identification is multifaceted. Post-modern conservatives may see themselves predominantly as members of a Western Civilization under attack by those who are sapping its "confidence." Often this is given an agonistic dimension, as these internal enemies are making it more challenging to combat external opponents affiliated with a different civilizational enemy, usually Islam. They may see themselves as belonging to the authentic ethnicity and culture of a given state, which is currently being dismantled through multi-culturalism, social fragmentation, and push for inclusion by untraditional groups such as LGBTQ and Trans individuals. Or in their most insidious variants, such as the white nationalism of alt-right founder Richard Spencer, they may sse themselves as belonging to a race currently under threat of demographic marginalization by minority groups who do ono look like them.

The identity or identities that the post-modern conservative affiliates with is usually one which has traditionally been at the top of its relevant social hierarchy; whether that be the "West" and the rest of the world, individuals who profess adherence to European culture contra others, or white people and the other "races." This persists in spite of the fact that each of these identities is highly vague and open to contention and change. But what remains a constant feature for the post-modern conservative is that the identity or identities they associate with are now under attack. The agonistic dimension of identity is a defining feature of the post-modern conservative narrative. These traditionally powerful groups are now being upended by enemies who seek to supplant them at the top of the social hierarchy. Often these enemies take two forms. The first are internal enemies: leftists, elitists, the media and so on who undermine the "confidence" of those belonging to traditionally powerful identities. And the second are external enemies. Usually these are lumped into even broader categories than the first: Islam, globalists, a Jewish conspiracy, "rootless cosmopolitans," freeloading allies and of course, Canada. As I will soon indicate in my Fifth point, these enemies are usually subject to rhetoric about a future crackdown which can materialize when post-modern conservatives take power.

Some might argue that this characterization seems all over the place, even vague. But as I will indicate, this vagueness and lack of ideological consistency is a definitive, even strategic, feature of post-modern conservatism.

3. *A contradictory and reactionary political ideology*

Political scientists and theorists often consider contradiction to be a fundamental weakness. This is because they are assessing a given ideology and believe that its logical coherence is connected to its concrete plausibility as a doctrine. But this emphasis on coherence misunderstands that contradiction can be an exceptionally powerful feature of a given ideology. The demand for coherence means that a political ideology can be invalidated and even refuted. When that ceases to be a concern, one is effectively enabled to believe whatever one wishes. It is hard to think of a more attractive selling point to individuals who feel that their identity is under attack.

The ideology of the post-modern conservative is a mess. As indicated, the post-modern dismissal of traditional standards for interpreting facts and values means that often its spokesmen make specious and untrue claims about facts. But even the narratives underpinning post-modern conservatism are unusual. On the one hand, the traditionally powerful identities with which they affiliate are strong enough to warrant their place on top of the social hierarchy. On the other, their strength is not sufficient to prevent the onslaught of terrifying and omnipresent enemies who are apparently now the "establishment" or the "ruling class" from upending them and becoming the dominant group in society. These enemies, both internal and external, are simultaneously regarded as omnipresent and exceptionally strong while also being weak, effeminate, and "losers." In the words of Umberto Eco, they are both too strong and too weak.

They are the Hollywood starlet and her allies the Latin American refugees and children all at once. Postmodern conservatives claim to hate identity politics and the victimization they associate with it, but of course continuously demand change by claiming victim status for their aggrieved identity.

This ideological inconsistency also applies to the materials used to justify the positions of postmodern conservatism. Sometimes they appeal to the alleged findings of the natural sciences to justify hierarchy, and claim to be simply "rational" about social issues. Sometimes they make sentimental appeals to tradition and its values. And sometimes, in a twist of Nietzschian irony, post-modern conservative atheists call for the retention of "cultural Christianity"--Christendom without Christ one might say.

These contradictions explain the extraordinary appeal of post-modern conservatism to its supporters. With demands for coherence out of the way, they can embrace all things and none. They are at once the strongest people in the world, and victims of a tremendously powerful conspiracy to overthrow them. Their enemies are at once elites who don't understand the average person, and losers and "libtards" who can't rise to the top of the social hierarchy. They despise post-modernism, but can embrace all the characteristics associated with the culture. It also enables them to be selective about which standards for knowledge and values they will respect one day or another. As I already indicated, the concern is not to move closer to the truth, whatever that is. It is to support the narrative the identity is oriented around. This is vastly enabled by the hyper-real mediums which are the breeding grounds of post-modern conservatism.

4. *Despite being reactionaries, post-modern conservatives deploy hyper-modern media to promulgate their political ideology*

One of the most unusual and unreflective aspects of post-modern conservatism has been its wholehearted embrace of new technological mediums to promulgate its worldview. This seems to have been done under the expectation that mediums are simply tools that convey the same message regardless of their specific dimensions. But this is highly idealistic. Technological mediums are not simply neutral, especially when it comes to communication. As the prophet of the post-modern epoch,Marshall McLuhan,put it: "The medium is the message." When we communicate through television, radio, and tweets on the internet this fundamentally changes the content we espouse and how it is received. These transformations were also well noted in Neil Postman's prophetic work *Amusing Ourselves to Death.* Postman argued that with the advent of television, modern people were gradually losing their ability to think through complex information the way they had when inhabiting a highly literate print civilization. This is because new mediums such as television are inclined to present complex issues by encapsulating them in a five minute soundbite. The immense competition for attention and views also meant that the entertainment value of the information had to be upped, increasing the temptation to give it a hyperbolic and partisan spin.

Post-modern conservatism is right at home with such social transformations. This is in spite of the fundamental paradox that employing hyper-modern mediums to defend conservatism will transform society in a way that is incompatible with conservative principles. The attraction is too strong since the agonistic vision of post-modern conservatism fits in nicely on the internet, where nuance is rare, attention short, and the demand for entertainment and spectacle unprecedented. This inclines even traditional conservative commentators to frame their presentations for a digital audience, giving it a distinctly post-modern twist. Complex matters get boiled down into "Peterson OWNS Feminist" and "Laughing at Stupid Things Liberals Say." This reinforces a dualistic vision of the world, amplifying partisanship, the sense of victimization, and the lust to vent social aggression to warrant attention and praise. These new mediums also increasingly operate as communication bubbles, enabling likeminded individuals to come together and increasingly isolate themselves from contact with other worldviews. Faced with a constant bombardment of post-modern conservative rhetoric, and encouraged by the community, this brings me to my fifth point.

5. *Once in power, post-modern conservatives actively crack down on other identity groups. Uniquely, this includes those who hold other epistemic and meta-ethical standards in order to preserve the hollow integrity of the victim narrative and its consequent political ideology. This leads to the perpetuation of the post-modern culture which birthed them in the first place. It is also coupled with calls for the effacement of traditional institutional and ideological barriers to the realization of the post-modern conservative political program*

Post-modern conservatism originated in many humble places, though many of its novelties have their origin in hyper-real mediums. However it has since seized power in countries such as the United States, Hungary, and the United Kingdom via the Brexit movement, and has begun instituting an agenda that enables us to assess what its politics will look like in real time. Post-modern conservatism's s ideology tends to be a mish mash of contradictions which makes it difficult to predict, but in practice there tends to be some consistency. Post-modern conservatives reject institutions and norms affiliated with globalization, desire greater state control of the economy, and seek to limit the intrusion of external "enemies" who will threaten the dominant identity they seek to restore to its rightful place. This necessitates cracking down on immigration, especially on groups arbitrarily regarded as deviating from the identities with which they affiliate.

But post-modern conservatism has a more insidious and novel characteristic as well. This flows from its dissolving the distinction between truth and falsity at an ideological level. In practice this means attacking and undermining the credibility of institutions which could counter the narrative of the administration and the identity politics it advocates. This can mean spreading doubt and engendering irrational skepticism about well verified and substantiated facts and norms. It can mean defunding or marginalizing alternative sources of knowledge which rely on the traditional standards. And in some extreme cases, it can mean outright banning of the expression of alternative narratives, as Victor Orban has done. This last possibility is the most worrying, as it would mean post-modern conservatism is firmly linking itself with the right wing authoritarianism of the past.

Part I

The Intellectual Origins of Post-Modern Conservatism

What is the Post-Modern Epoch?

Matt McManus

Why the Shift to the Post-Modern Epoch?

"In contemporary society and culture – post-industrial society, postmodern culture - the question of the legitimation of knowledge is formulated in different terms. The grand narrative has lost its credibility, regardless of what mode of unification it uses, regardless of whether it is a speculative narrative or a narrative of emancipation."

Jean Francois Lyotard, *The Post-Modern Condition*

To understand post-modern conservatism, which is the primary purpose of this book, it is essential to have some understanding of what post-modernism itself is. I believe that post-modernism is best understood as an epoch in the history of developed societies; one characterized by specific material, socio-cultural, and communicative practices. This situates my position in a long line of thinkers who've approached post-modernism in much the same way. Here I will give an overview of their general positions. Those who argue that post-modernism is an epoch in the history of developed societies often approach the subject in a very different way than its philosophical proponents. While they would often agree that ours is a more skeptical time, these thinkers were keen to analyze and then criticize the immense transformations that underpinned this shift. Perhaps inevitably, these thinkers who regard post-modernism as an epoch vary widely in their theoretical and political diagnoses.

Marxist critics like Frederic Jameson, David Harvey, and Mark Fisher lay the blame for the emergence of post-modern culture at the feet of "late capitalism" or "neoliberalism," arguing that the penetration of capitalist market forces into our communal and personal lives has revolutionized the way we think and communicate with one another. For Frederic Jameson, post-modernism is a stage in late capitalism where we increasingly stop creating new artistic and cultural forms. Instead we transform our own past and history into a pastiche of entertaining but often spectral commodities. Take Indiana Jones. Ancient biblical tropes would be combined with imagery from the 1930s filtered through the format of a 1950s serial. Or consider The Avengers. Ancient Norse Gods would fight alongside Cold War era spies and super soldiers from the Second World War. For David Harvey, neoliberal capitalism is always physically destroying the society around it to erect a new one in its place. Local businesses are torn down for strip malls, strip malls give way to shopping centers, and shopping centers give way to Amazon warehouses. This continuous transformation of the environment we live within is immensely destabilizing and is associated with consequent transformations in how we move about, communicate, and labor. Lastly, Mark Fisher argues that the end of history increasingly generated the sense that there was no real alternative to capitalist social systems. This in turn resulted in a growing cultural stagnation. Individuals increasingly realize there are no more great political, ideological, and spiritual battles to be fought. So we now endlessly recycle the past, creating pastiches out of the religious, literary, and political ideologies of York to provide some distraction from our frozen existence.

Conservative critics like Allan Bloom and Patrick Deneen have a different, more classical approach to understanding what I call "post-modern culture." For Bloom, post-modern culture emerged as a consequence of social decadence. Universities increasingly turned from their mission to inculcate youth into the traditions of old. Instead they now promote a vulgar identity politics in the humanities, which themselves are now continuously squeezed to send more students into the various STEM fields which uncritically propagated the cultural status quo while driving forward technological and economic innovations. This is coupled with a vulgar and banal entertainment industry, which produces unchallenging and easily digestible entertainment as a substitute to developing genuinely edifying art. This results in a declining sense of virtue and intellectual energy amongst the young. Patrick Deneen's account of post-modern culture is even more radical. He argues that the emergence of post-modern culture can be traced back to liberalism itself. Liberalism unleashed an individualistic and self-interested culture in which people focused so much on the pursuit of their individual needs and related private truths that they abandoned the connections to one another necessary to preserve a commitment to communal truths. Deneen's argument is fascinating, and those interested in learning more are welcome to look at my overview of his seminal new book *Why Liberalism Failed*.

Another group of figures who discussed the advent of post-modern culture were media and communication theorists like Guy Debord, Jean Baudrillard, and Neil Postman. They followed the ever prophetic Marshall McLuhan, who argued that we had long misunderstood technologies and media as little more than the tools we used in the pursuit of given ends. This was simply wrong-headed, as McLuhan understood that the tools we use eventually start using and shaping us.

This interest in technology and new mediums was picked up by many media and communication theorists concerned with the emergence of post-modern culture. For Guy Debord, "all that was once directly lived has become mere representation." As modern technologies develop, we increasingly do not interact with one another on a one to one basis. Instead we understand our communal lives in terms of symbols and imagery; news feeds which appear on television, Facebook memes fomenting political partisanship, Twitter rants by the President and so on. The result is an increasing inability to interact with other people, and with our community, in an authentic way. We also lose our ability to distinguish between symbols and reality. Neil Postman made many of the same points. For Postman, our formerly literary culture was being replaced with one where most of the information we imbibed was received through mediums like television, radio, and of course, computers. This increased the volume of information we were capable of perceiving at any given moment, while often gutting it of substance. In our new post-modern culture, most citizens were exposed to so many sources of information, they were forced to compete with one another for attention and controversy. This had the result of eroding traditional mediums for transmitting information, like books and newspapers, which analyzed given topics at length and in depth. Instead we were exposed to five minute soundbites with the pretension of summarizing complex political positions, YouTube lectures summarizing "post-modern neo-Marxism" in the time it takes to get a coffee, and so on.

And finally, there is Jean Baudrillard, a writer of genius. Baudrillard argued that our "hyper-real" era was increasingly defined by the rule of symbols. As we increasingly plugged into an ever greater number of new mediums, the division between the real and the unreal, the simulacra and the simulacrum, dissolved. For people in many developed countries even war, the most paradigmatically "real" phenomenon, increasingly became understood and interpreted through hyper-real simulated mediums. Consider the recent strike with "the mother of all bombs"; annihilation presented as WWE style entertainment presided over by the Donald: the post-modern conservative President who made his name in reality television and whose image always threatens to overwhelm his abyssal reality. For Baudrillard, the result of these technological changes was our increasing transformation into well connected automatons; informed on everything but interested in nothing, flat and "one dimensional" beings concerned with image and spectacle over dialogue and reflection. The world is not becoming meaningless, it is becoming so saturated with symbolism that meaning itself no longer means anything. Substance had now finally given way to triumphant form. As Baudrillard put it:

"Everywhere one seeks to produce meaning, to make the world signify, to render it visible. We are not, however, in danger of lacking meaning; quite the contrary, we are gorged with meaning and it is killing us."

Conclusion: The Shift from the Modern to the Post-Modern Epoch

"What does a scanner see? he asked himself. I mean, really see? Into the head? Down into the heart? Does a passive infrared scanner like they used to use or a cube-type holo-scanner like they use these days, the latest thing, see into me - into us - clearly or darkly? I hope it does, he thought, see clearly, because I can't any longer these days see into myself. I see only murk. Murk outside; murk inside. I hope, for everyone's sake, the scanners do better. Because, he thought, if the scanner sees only darkly, the way I myself do, then we are cursed, cursed again and like we have been continually, and we'll wind up dead this way, knowing very little and getting that little fragment wrong too."

Philip K Dick, *A Scanner Darkly*

Each of the thinkers discussed above had a different interpretation of why the post-modern epoch emerged. For the Marxists, it is primarily the dynamics of neoliberal capitalist society which are to blame. For many conservative critics, it is growing cultural decadence and the transformation of social institutions which traditionally inculcated virtue, such as universities and the artistic industries, into cheapened versions of themselves hawking paltry wares. And for many of the critics in media and communication studies, post-modern culture emerged as the result of profound technological transformations which have fundamentally changed the way we communicate and interact, often for the worse.

I believe that we have much more to learn from those who regard post-modernism as an epoch than from those who offer post-modern philosophies. This is in part because post-modern culture is increasingly becoming an explicit topic of concern in the public sphere, and rightly so. With the emergence of post-modern conservatism as a major and vulgar political force, it becomes more necessary than ever to probe into the roots of our culture and how to abet its most dangerous tendencies. I will not conclude here by suggesting which of the approaches discussed above is most useful for these purposes.

It is difficult to pinpoint when the shift from modernism to post-modernism occurred. As I have already observed in the last article, the culture and politics of the late 19th and early 20th centuries were already marked by growing distrust of authority and increasing skepticism that human reason could lead us to anything like certainty. The Great Depression and the Second World War were cataclysmic events that shook the faith of many developed societies, particularly the overweening hubris that they were destined to always enjoy not just a technological, but a moral, superiority over other cultures. The paranoia of the Cold War and the prospect of nuclear annihilation, coupled with growing cynicism and disdain towards corrupt political figures like Joseph McCarthy, Charles De Gaulle, and Richard Nixon also played their role in fostering distrust and a sense of unreality.

But I speculate that the real moment post-modern culture became explicitly understood was with the publication of Phillip K. Dick's 1959 novel *Time Out of Joint*. Dick's protagonist Ragle Gumm believes he is living in an idyllic, if boring, American suburb in 1959. He later learns that the town is a simulated reality designed to prevent him from realizing the dark political truth that Ragle was living in the 1990s and that the earth was at war with colonists it had mistreated. This seemingly pulpish science fiction story was amongst the first works to truly exhibit the features that would come to be associated with post-modern culture. Ragle seemed to be living in a 1950s United States that was at the height of its affluence, stability, and traditionalism. But this world was a lie concealing the truth, and moreover, a dark truth about the past that could only be denied by pretending it was not already the future. And this is what characterizes the post-modern epoch: growing skepticism about everything around us masked by an unwillingness to realize that the seemingly stable world we think we live in has already been dated and disposed of through immense processes of social, economic, and technological transformation.

Post-Modern Conservatism: Or How the Right Became What it Hated

Introduction

Few things rile up today's conservatives like the boogeyman of post-modernism. Associated with identity politics, political correctness, social justice warriors, and relativistic cultural Marxism, post-modernism is often degraded as the locus of everything that is wrong with society. Jordan Peterson, now a right wing hero, has characterized it as "dangerous" and "radical." The National Security Council claimed post-modern "cultural Marxism" was at the root of opposition to Trump. And Ben Shapiro, not to be outdone, called Obama the first "post-modern" President. Where, one might ask, does all this hatred come from?

The Right on Post-Modernism

The root of most conservative critiques of post-modernism are its alleged attacks on the idea of universal truth. In lieu of believing that there are universal scientific and moral truths that apply everywhere and to everyone, regardless of their background, critics claim that post-modernism leads to the belief that everything is dependent on social context. This leads to the belief that, rather than being singular, truth is fundamentally pluralistic. What counts as truth for a wealthy white male like Donald Trump might not count as truth for a black single mother living in Chicago. This, it is claimed, leads quickly to the kind of identity politics and politically correct culture prominently associated with the Left. Since there are no universal truths to which everyone is beholden, identity becomes singularly important since it is now the locus for what we think and why. This means that identity becomes the primary driver behind politics as different groups compete to have their identity-specific truths reflected in the law and social behavior.

This conservative account has always been more of a superficial caricature of post-modern thought than an accurate description. For the most part, it seems derived from a desire to clamp down on the scourge of campus politics-surely the most pressing social issue today!-than any thorough look at post-modern thought. There is little in this account of post-modernism, for example, that would be recognizable to Derrida, Foucault, Lyotard or any of the other major authors in the tradition. But my point isn't to criticize conservatives for getting post-modernism wrong. My point, rather, is that not recognizing that many conservatives have started to move closer and closer to the ideology and stereotypes of the very post-modernism they claim to criticize. In other words, we are witnessing the emergence of post-modern conservatism.

Post-Modern Conservatism

Contrary to popular belief, identity politics and a distrust of truth is hardly foreign to conservatism. The great English conservative thinker Edmund Burke made his name asserting the primacy of cultural identity and tradition over the hyper rationalism of the elite intellectuals who brought about the French Revolution. Echoing today's anti-elitism, Burke worried that the age of chivalry and respect for tradition was coming to an end, replaced by the age of "sophisters, economists, and calculators." Burke was followed in these sentiments by generations of conservative thinkers, from Oakeshott to Robert Bork, arguing that conservatism promotes identity, history and particularity against the rationalism and universalism of arrogant liberals. Or as the British Lord Devlin put it when opposing support for gay rights against the claims of the liberal H.L.A Hart, society should accept the values "the man on the Clapham omnibus" would accept. Not because they are right. But because his identity is reflective of the national identity.

Today's post-modern conservatives are the (often) unknowing heirs to this tradition, but par usual, have radicalized it. These promotors of "alternative facts" are like their left wing cousins in arguing for a kind of identity politics against the universalism of modern values. But where left wing post-modernism argues that we need a society that respects a plurality of different identities, post-modern conservatives want a return to a singular national identity. Post-modern conservatism claims that the Left has marginalized people who hold to the traditional and legitimate "truths," and that this this is deeply wrong. Not because there are better arguments or reasons for these "truths" than any others. Post-modern conservatism is characterized by its disdain for intellectual authority, preferring ties of identity and commonality. Because these "truths" are those that historically held society together.

In practice, this means that post-modern conservatives have mobilized their identity to push for a retrenchment of traditional values against the demands of both classical liberals who believe in the objective truth of liberalism, and post-modern leftists who want a more pluralistic society. The rise of Donald Trump, the identity politics of Brexit and the French National Front, and the development of "illiberal democracy" in Hungary and Poland, are all symptoms of the right's embrace of post-modern tropes. These political actors and movements demonstrate contempt for their opponents. They affiliate with people who think, look, and talk like them, and are wary of outsiders who don't share that identity. And above all else, they are dismissive of possible "truths" that don't accord with tradition and "common sense," calling them "fake news" and other cute neologisms. In other words, they've become what they claimed to hate. We're all the poorer for it.

What is Post-Modern Conservatism

Matt McManus

Irrationalism, The Political Right and Collective Identities

Many on the Left maintain that, in contrast to conservatives, we must have greater respect for difference. Conservatives are seen as supporting a universalistic and moralizing vision of the world, backed up by the power of capital, the ideological heft of liberalism, and the martial strength of Western hegemons like the United States and the United Kingdom. These forces operate to quash difference at home and crush it abroad, spreading markets through the power of globalization and world institutions while destroying different systems of economic organization, and promoting a universal liberal individualism as the only viable ideology.

All of this helps explain the attraction of post-modernism to the Left. With its rejection of objective truth and morals and all the grand narratives they hold up, to its interest in demonstrating the equal validity of other ways of knowing and expressing, post-modernism must have seemed like a breath of fresh air. But the ground has shifted. Conservative movements have been able to assimilate the lessons of post-modernism and synthesize them with older reactionary philosophies. In many ways, conservatives have been more successful in this respect than the Left ever was, in part because post-modern conservatives have never been concerned about enthusiastically embracing the paradoxical consequences of their positions.

To understand how this can be so, we must look back to older and more particularistic forms of conservatism. These precedents demonstrate that post-modern conservatism didn't emerge in an intellectual and cultural vacuum. Post-Modernism and a certain type of conservatism found each other because they were a natural fit for one another.

Perhaps the most important predecessor of post-modern conservatism is Edmund Burke. In his *Reflections on the Revolution in France,* Burke famously condemned the French Revolutionaries, those innovators with "a selfish temper and confined views." He was deeply hostile not just to their political views, but to the haughty rationalism which seemed to underpin them. Burke criticized the belief that society could be transformed from the ground up according to some pretentious scheme which claimed to be based on a fully rational philosophy. In a populist vein, Burke railed against the "solitude of metaphysical abstraction" that led to dangerous and violent radicalism. For instance, Burke believed that the abstract rights of man coveted by the Revolutionaries could never be achieved except by destroying the venerable institutions which worked to counter the impulses of those who thought they knew better than their ancestors.

Burke never quite slipped into endorsing the outright irrationalism we see today amongst post-modern conservatives. But he laid the groundwork for irrationalism's assimilation into later branches of conservatism. Burke was deeply skeptical that there was an objective truth and set of morals which could be discovered or constructed through the power of human reason and applied to all societies at all times. One can see his influence on conservatives throughout the ages. For instance, in "Rationalism and Politics" Michael Oakeshott famously argued that modern people must choose between a nihilistic commitment to a rationalist politics, or embrace the irrational but far more satisfying commitment to one's culture and society based on a habit of "affection and behavior" rather than self-reflection and calculation. Burke's irrationalism also colors the work of conservative legalists like Robert Bork, who in *Coercing Virtue: The Worldwide Rule of Judges* famously denounced Leftists for having little respect for "particularity-respect for difference, circumstance, history, and the irreducible complexity of human beings and human societies," and Antonin Scalia who claimed that the goal of American law was to express "skepticism that evolving standards of decency always meant progress and that societies always mature as opposed to rot."

These intellectual precedents demonstrate why the shift to post-modern positions was not, despite its long association with the Left, an unparalleled leap for conservatives. The ground had long been laid in the veneration of irrationalism and the consequent focus on culture and society over reason and objectivity.

Contemporary Post-Modern Conservatism

Post-modern conservatism echoes many of the same points as its irrationalist predecessors, but exacerbates their most extreme tendencies. Post-modern conservatism is also backed up by the tremendous power of modern technology and capital.

Ironically, post-modern conservatism, as it manifests on radio, in blogs, and websites, is often superficially hostile towards what it takes as the tenets of post-modernism and "cultural Marxism" (whatever the latter means). It is dismissive of historical accounts of racism and genocide by Western powers. It disdains social context. And most obviously, post-modern conservatism is paranoid about any criticisms of Western civilization and its values. But these surface conflicts belie the deeper unity between the post-modernism and post-modern conservatism. The most intense political conflicts are almost always between two groups who operate within similar ideological frameworks. Post-modern conservatism is post-modern because it disdains belief in objective truth and mores, whether offered by science or of social science, and locates meaning in a reactionary identity and its values. This is expressed in post-modern conservatism's approach to politics. Since there is no objective truth to be found, there are no firm criteria for mediating between or evaluating the truth of different value systems and policies. Facts can be countered by appeal to alternative facts. Critics can be dismissed as fake news. What matters for post-modern conservatives is remaining faithful to a conservative identity.

Post-modern conservatism is ascendant across the Anglo-Saxon world, as manifested in the election of the Pynchonesque Donald Trump, and the Brexit decision of the United Kingdom. It has worryingly bubbled to the surface in the civilizational nationalism of Marine Le-Pen, the xenophobic political-theology of Geert Wilders, and the Crusader mentality of the Law and Justice Party of Poland. Each of these movements and parties has abandoned the conservative universalism and turned inward. Post-modern conservative movements and parties have adopted the rhetoric and symbolism of a reactionary identity. Sometimes they link with likeminded conservatives in states belonging to "Western Civilization," sometimes they keep things at the level of a crude nationalism. In each case, post-modern conservative movements and parties rely on alienation and resentment, rather than facts and argument, to push an agenda critical of globalization, integration, and universalistic movements. The old universalistic conservative stalwarts, embodied by figures dead-William Buckley- and living - Nicolas Sarkozy- are being rudely swept aside for their conformity and alleged support for a globalizing order. They are being replaced by figures who are relativistic, dismissive or even ignorant of the idea of truth, and consequently, all the more aggressive in using the technologies that facilitated their rise to push a transparently ideological agenda. To the extent that post-modern conservatives have achieved political success, whether through seizing power or advancing policies, they have changed both the substance and form of politics.

The Rise and Emergence of Post-Modern Conservatism

Matt McManus

Introduction

Few things agitate today's intellectually informed conservatives and classical liberals like post-modern theory and its concretization in identity politics. In a *National Review* article, Victor Hanson of the Hoover Institute related post-modernism to "poison," and decried falling standards of "truth and falsity." Jordan Peterson has characterized post-modernism as dangerous, and identity politics as a kind of self-pitying victimization. In my home country of Canada, Rex Murphy of the right-leaning *National Post* has characterized movements oriented around identity politics as "intolerant" and their participants as a "mob." In Britain, Roger Scruton has accused post-modern intellectuals of destroying "high culture" by effacing aesthetic standards. And the litany goes on. It would be impossible to summarize the content of all these varied criticisms here. Instead, I will summarize them before moving on to discussing the emergence of post-modern conservatism and identity politics. The locus of many conservative criticisms of post-modernism seems to be twofold.

Firstly, conservatives are concerned with the theoretical consequences of post-modern theory. In less sophisticated critiques, conservatives decry post-modernism for undermining belief in traditional epistemological and moral standards. These criticisms are not especially powerful, since they are largely predicated on a nostalgic desire to hold on to those specific standards regardless of their tenability. Indeed, most of them take the form of demanding adherence to tradition for the sake of stability, rather than that tradition's inner truth and value.

The most sophisticated critique, offered amongst others by Allan Bloom in his seminal book *The Closing of the American Mind*, is more tenable. Bloom and his disciples are less concerned that post-modern theorists undermine this or that theory of truth. After all, Western philosophers and scientists have been engaging in critical activities since at least Socrates. What Bloom was concerned about was that post-modern theorists seemed indifferent to the entire possibility of truth, dismissing it as an outdated and even dangerous idea. For Bloom, this was a travesty, since it led to the gradual diminishing of the individual spirit, as each person nihilistically came to take their own private satisfactions and opinions as determinate in all epistemic and moral circumstances. He thought this would be disastrous for all involved.

Secondly, conservatives are concerned with what they consider the concrete consequences of adhering to post-modern theory: a belief in identity politics. For these critics, identity politics is the logical consequence of adherence to the aforementioned theoretical positions. Once one takes one's own private satisfactions and opinions as the locus for all epistemological and moral judgments, it makes one's identity and its perceived oppressors incredibly significant. Moreover, this focus on identity and oppression leads to the understanding that everything is ultimately about power and who has it. Knowledge, venerable institutions, politics, and the economy are all conceived as forces which systematically oppress and repress the expression of one's identity. Since this expression is taken as both the source for all legitimate knowledge and value, this is regarded as a very great wrong. The individual's efforts then become directed against both removing these systems of oppression and placing one's self, and the group one affiliates with, on top of the power hierarchy. This leads to activism which is highly oppressive and totalitarian, since its aim is not the classical liberal goal of convincing others through reason and discourse. Rather, it is to replace one powerful group with another.

What is Post-Modernism?

I believe there is something to these criticisms of post-modern discourse, though they are not without their limitations. As Nathan J. Robinson of *Current Affairs* put it, there has been a notable unwillingness on the part of many conservative and classical liberal thinkers to actually engage with post-modern ideas and identity-politics activists in a significant way. This has led to a considerable amount of intellectual vagueness. For instance, in his recent *Twelve Rules for Life,* Jordan Peterson accuses Jacques Derrida of committing many of the theoretical and concrete sins highlighted above. However, he does not cite any major work by the French iconoclast. Frankly, it shows, since the version of Derrida he confronts is closer to a caricature than a fleshed out intellectual rival. Then there is the pervasive tendency to characterize post-modern identity activists as "cultural Marxists." This demonstrates a serious misunderstanding of both Marxism and post-modernism. Generalizing very broadly, the former was highly committed to an almost Messianic theory of truth, had scientific pretensions for historical materialism as a doctrine, and was concerned with truth inhibiting ideology rather than truth effacing "power." The latter had a complex relationship to truth, rejected historical materialism and indeed scientism (if not science), and was concerned to show that behind power there was only more power.

Generally speaking, left wing authors who wrote about post-modernism divided into two respective lines of thought. Some of them were actually quite critical. Firstly, there were largely Marxist and post-Marxist scholars like Frederic Jameson, David Harvey, Jean Francois Lyotard, Neil Postman and Jean Baudrillard who understood post-modernism as an epoch in Western history. They claimed that a combination of economic, technological, and social changes had brought about an epoch where individuals were increasingly skeptical and disinterested in epistemological and moral "grand narratives." They saw these as anachronistic features of the past of little concern in consumer culture. To the extent that they were concerned with epistemological or moral issues, this was largely driven by a desire for self-satisfaction in a market context. Individuals in the post-modern epoch learned about knowledge and morals because this information was a tool to get ahead in a market context. Interestingly enough, these leftist critics of post-modernism share a great deal in common with conservative critics like the aforementioned Allan Bloom and the University of Notre Dame's Patrick Deneen. These authors also see post-modernism as an epoch, established by social factors, which results in treating knowledge and morals as little more than a consumerist toolkit.

The second school line of thinking in left wing post-modernism is closer to the caricature lambasted by conservative critics, though even here we must be careful. Authors in this second line of thought were at the very least skeptical about the possibility of establishing firm epistemic and moral frameworks that would allow us uninhibited access to the world. Moreover, they did not regard these epistemic and moral conclusions as contingent on epochal social circumstances. They regarded them as philosophical "conclusions" (though of course not truths!) that were paradoxically valid for all time. Moreover, many of them did indeed regard power-whether authorial power, institutional power, or disciplinary power-as responsible for giving strong epistemic and moral truth claims and undeserved validity. Representative authors in this line of thinking include Michel Foucault, Jacques Derrida, Bruno Latour, and America's own Richard Rorty. Now it is important to qualify these observations by noting that none of these authors outright rejected the idea of truth wholesale. Each qualified their skepticism by appealing to different principles, whether it be faith on the part of Derrida, or American pragmatism for Richard Rorty. But they did indeed offer important-if I think ultimately unconvincing-problems for those who have strong beliefs about the truth of knowledge and morals.

Ultimately I am inclined to sympathizing with the former line of authors rather than the latter. This includes intelligent conservative critics of post-modernism such as Patrick Deneen and Bloom. I believe that post-modern positions emerged in our current epoch due to a complex array of social forces. The authors in the second line of left wing post-modern commentators drew inspiration from these social forces to formulate interesting, but ultimately flawed philosophies which will not stand the test of time when evaluated from a purely intellectual standpoint. But this is not my major concern here. If post-modern positions emerge as a consequence of social forces, this presents a more general problem for critics of post-modernism generally. It is not simply the fact that a number of skeptical university professors are professing flawed philosophical positions, and thence inspiring individuals to take radical political positions on identity and power as a consequence. Instead, post-modern positions can emerge in a variety of places when individuals are effected by the social forces of the epoch in the right way. This is what I believe accounts for the emergence of post-modern conservatism.

The Intellectual Origins of Post-Modern Conservatism

The association of conservatism with a strong commitment to epistemic and moral truth, both in general and regarding particular doctrines, is far more contingent and ahistorical than some partisans may expect. In fact there is a long history in conservative and other right wing circles of rejecting strong epistemic and moral truths. As highlighted by Leo Strauss in his seminal *Natural Right and History,* the modern origins of this right wing rejection of epistemic and moral truths are in the work of Edmund Burke. Burke was staunchly critical of the abstract intellectualism of the French revolutionaries, and their desire to rationalize society. Against abstract and scientific approaches to knowledge and morality, Burke emphasized the need to pay close attention to history, tradition, and the identity of a particular people. As Strauss observed, much of this is sound advice and dire warning to fundamentalists of all stripes. But it also constitutes a shift towards regarding knowledge and morality as contingent upon particular circumstances and histories. This tendency to associate revolutionary progressivism with abstract respect for reason continued in the thought of right wing thinkers like Joseph De Maistre, hailed by Isaiah Berlin as the intellectual predecessor of "fascism." De Maistre argued that the human capacity to reason towards true knowledge and morals was so fundamentally limited it needed to be massively supplemented by faith in traditional authorities and revealed religion. He was a reactionary of the highest pitch, damning the French Revolutionaries for their arrogant conceit of having figured the world out for themselves, and demanding a return to the values of throne and altar.

In the modern era, there have been plenty of conservative thinkers who have also condemned rationalism, upholding the value of tradition and history as a relative source of knowledge and morals. Michael Oakeshott's famed essay "Rationalism in Politics" argued that what defines a conservative is respect for the epistemic and moral authority of tradition over abstract faith in the power of Utilitarian reason. In his debate with H.L.A Hart, conservative Lord Devlin justified restrictions on homosexuality by claiming that true morality is a matter of what the "man on the Clapham omnibus" believed. Justice Robert Bork, Reagan's favored pick for the Supreme Court, wrote in *Coercing Virtue* that what characterized the left wing "new class" was its belief in universal values and truths. Instead, conservatives were defined by their veneration of "particularity-respect for difference, circumstance, (and) history..." He condemned this progressive "new class" for attempting to push its pretentious universalistic ideas about knowledge and morals onto traditionally oriented societies which did not want them.

My point here is not to accuse any of these authors of holding to specifically post-modern doctrines. Nor do I want to accuse them of being responsible for the emergence of what I call "post-modern conservatism." As I mentioned before, I believe post-modernism emerged as a result of social factors particular to our epoch. It was not driven primarily by intellectual shifts; intellectual shifts were driven by post-modern culture. My point is to observe that the association of conservatism with a strong commitment to truth is contingent rather than consistent throughout history. In a highly radicalized and even mutilated form, the ideas developed by the above authors provide an intellectual backdrop for explaining why many conservatives increasingly look like their left post-modern "adversaries," right down to their commitment to identity politics.

Conclusion: The Emergence of Post-Modern Conservatism

What fundamentally characterizes post-modern conservatives is locating epistemic and moral authority in a given traditional identity. Post-modern conservatism is a highly radicalized iteration of the intellectual movements indicated above, often emerging in periods of economic and social crisis and finding initial expression in hyper-modern mediums such as the internet. Post-modern conservatives increasingly regard strong truth claims about knowledge and morality with active suspicion and even hostility. This is because they regard the intellectual and cultural "elites" who produce knowledge and popularize moral norms as progressive, abstract, and unlikely to sympathize with their concerns. Rather than attempting to formulate alternative claims about knowledge and morality which might have some epistemic and meta-ethical tenability, post-modern conservatives reject even these standards. Instead they largely appeal to identity as the locus for epistemic and moral validity. This is in turn used to rally political support for a given agenda designed to restore that identity to power.

In this respect, post-modern conservatives are not substantially different from their left wing "adversaries." Both regard identity as the locus of epistemic and moral validity, and both are concerned to achieve power since that is the only major concern. Some post-modern conservatives, notably Dennis Prager, have even gone so far as to declare conservatives as being in the midst of a "civil war" with the left over what identity is going to become hegemonic across society. The difference between the two is a matter of emphasis. Left wing post-modern identity politics tends to be concerned with overturning the power of traditionally dominant groups. They direct their barbs against figures like white, heterosexual males, who are perceived as inherently oppressive. By contrast, right wing post-modern identity politics tends to be concerned with retrenching the power of traditionally dominant identity groups against these same assaults. In its less extreme form, it attacks the aforementioned "elites" who formulate knowledge and values regarded as hostile to traditionally dominant identity groups, dismissing their claims as "fake news" or contrasting their claims with "alternative facts." More extreme post-modern conservatives regard these elites as allied with immigrants, refugees and other individuals whose existence within the country poses the danger of social fragmentation and the further breakdown of tradition. This can occasionally lead them to express xenophobic and even racist sentiments.

Post-modern conservatives are now an ascendant group. President Donald Trump has attempted to dismantle the truth-telling apparatus of government, gutting funding and eliminating positions for scientists and technocrats who dissent from his views. The ruling Law and Justice Party of Poland has expressed concern about the "liquidation of the civilization that grew out of Christianity" and called for restrictive measures to prevent further changes. Viktor Orban of Hungary has criticized European elites for inviting immigrants into the country, leading to "changing values." In each case, these figures and parties challenge strong ideas about truth by appealing to traditionally dominant identities concerned about social changes promoted by elites and intellectuals. This should be deeply concerning to all, and demonstrates how the reach of the post-modern epoch has moved far beyond just influencing a few left wing radicals on university campuses.

The Decline of Conservativism: Post-Modern Culture and the Collapse of Traditionalism

Matt McManus

Introduction

In an article for *The New York Times,* conservative icon Roger Scruton lamented over "What Trump Doesn't Get About Conservativism." Scruton argues that Trump largely bypasses intellectual arguments about conservatism and principle when defending partially conservative policies. Scruton then goes on to characterize conservatism as being not about one "universal" doctrine, but about a variety of particular traditions. Conservatism is supporting specific people in a specific place who wish to conserve their particular tradition of being in the world. But, Scruton argues, the only way to successfully achieve this political goal is for politicians to "reform in order to conserve." This means enabling a sufficient level of prosperity to ensure that individuals are capable of upholding their specific traditions. He then goes on to argue that conservatives have long understood the virtues of free market capitalism in enabling the prosperity necessary to enjoy values in other traditional spheres of social endeavor:

"Conservative thinkers have on the whole praised the free market, but they do not think that market values are the only values there are. Their primary concern is with the aspects of society in which markets have little or no part to play: education, culture, religion, marriage and the family. Such spheres of social endeavor arise not through buying and selling but through cherishing what cannot be bought and sold: things like love, loyalty, art and knowledge, which are not means to an end but ends in themselves."

Scruton then goes on to criticize Trump's protectionist policies and sense of victimization for engendering a "cultural pessimism" symptomatic of a broader decline. Scruton regards Trump as symptomatic of the decline of Anglo-American culture and Western civilization more generally. The solution to this decline, or so Scruton claims elsewhere, is a return to classically conservative values such as support for the free market, and concern with spheres of social endeavor affiliated with traditionalism. Scruton's work fits nicely with those of other conservatives who have recognized Trumpism as antithetical to any genuine conservatism. This includes Patrick Deneen, who gestures to Trumpism as indication of a crisis of faith in the American Conservatism, Bill Kristol, and many others. For these figures, Trump and Trumpism represents a turn away from a conservatism sincerely concerned with preserving tradition and promoting the prosperity of the entire nation. Consequently, all traditionalist conservatives should push for the swift end of Trumpism.

I agree with many of these commentators that Trumpism is an aberration from traditionalist conservatism in many respects. I also share their belief that Trump's manifold vulgarities, his dissolution of the boundaries between truth and falsehood and the reckless myopia of his policies are dangerous and need to be stopped. But I think that many of these conservative commentators demonstrate a nostalgia for a traditionalist conservatism which is largely spent as a political force. While iterations of it may continue to exist, and even obtain power sporadically, traditionalist conservatism has become outdated by economic, social, and especially technological transformations. To the extent that it survives as a political force it will increasingly be as a hyper-real form of post-modern conservatism.

What Is Conservatism?

In the modern Anglo-American world, most political

conservatives a la Margaret Thatcher, Ronald Reagan, Stephen Harper, and David Cameron adopted an "ordered liberty" approach to social mores and combine this with a neo-liberal faith in capitalist markets as the guarantors of socio-economic prosperity. This has led some commentators to write as though this were the only form of conservatism at all conceivable. Nothing could be further from the truth. Conservativism is a complex political ideology with many different intellectual iterations. There is the Catholic traditionalism and communitarianism of Patrick Deneen and Alasdair Macintyre. There is the natural law conservatism of Leo Strauss, Harry Jaffa, and John Finnis. Democratic conservatives such as Robert Bork and Antonin Scalia grounded their conservatism in a belief that the "people" tend to dislike drastic change. And there is the tradition of liberal "ordered liberty" associated with Edmund Burke and Russell Kirk. The freedom loving neo-liberalism of Hayek and Friedman. The extreme irrationalism of Joseph De Maistre and the tempered pragmatism of Michael Oakeshott. And in its darker iterations, the virulent nationalism and totalitarianism of Carl Schmitt and Martin Heidegger. And so on.

These iterations of conservative thought vary and overlap widely in their philosophical arguments and substantive claims. Each has had an impact on politically conservative movements across the Western world. This ideological variety may seem intellectually overwhelming. But I believe Scruton is right that it is underwritten by a core belief shared by almost all conservatives that political power should be exercised to reform parts of society to conserve the traditions one can. Or as put by Michael Oakeshott: "To be conservative, then, is to prefer the familiar to the unknown, to prefer the tried to the untried, fact to mystery, the actual to the possible, the limited to the unbounded, the near to the distant, the sufficient to the superabundant, the convenient to the perfect, present laughter to utopian bliss." And would add, to be conservative is to use political power to conserve the familiar, the tried, and so on.

This brings me to the heart of the matter. To the extent that luminaries such as Scruton, Deneen, and Kristol criticize Trump it is for failing to live up to this basic conservative expectation, and in this they are correct. The presumption underpinning this conservative critique of Trump is that if he were to just vanish, one could return to the traditionalist conservatism of old. I do not think that is the case. The reason is that the post-modern culture which has developed operates at such a hyper-real level and transforms society with such speed and efficiency that it makes traditionalist conservatism increasingly outdated as a concrete political ideology and approach. As a result, old political ideologies are giving way to new post-modern iterations. Traditionalist conservatism is mutating into post-modern conservatism.

What Is Post-Modern Culture?

Post-modernism is often thrown around as the boogeyman of the right. Often badly mislabeled as "cultural Marxism," post-modernism is perhaps best understood in two interrelated ways. The first is more narrowly. Postmodernism can be understood as a skeptical philosophical position articulated in the work of thinkers such as Jacques Derrida and Michel Foucault. These thinkers developed complex theories regarding why it was unlikely that various forms of reason could ever lead us to absolute certainty about the way the world is and the way it should be. Often their arguments were brilliant, if not entirely novel, given that there is a long intellectual history in the West of being skeptical of truth, or arguing that power is the basis of knowledge. I am not primarily interested in unpacking their specific philosophical arguments here.

The second and more interesting way to understand post-modernism is as an epoch in human history. Or as I will characterize it here, as a culture. Post-modern culture is characterized by many different features. At an economic level, it is characterized by increasing global interconnectedness. Globalization brings the world together economically, facilitating the rapid and increasingly instantaneous transportation of goods from different cultures and traditions to alien environments. It also upsets traditional labor markets and industry, as the free movement of capital across the globe means dissolving ancient and local ways of producing and selling goods. These are replaced with vast interconnected webs of production, distribution, and consumption spread across the world. Much of this is driven by the internationalization of labor, as economic firms and laborers both become migratory while looking for ever greater opportunities. Underpinning much of this, is what liberal economist Joseph Schumpeter called the "creative destruction" of traditional values. To sell new commodities, economic firms create and market new value systems, and in so doing, tear down the old. This even includes religion, which as Patrick Deneen nicely points out, can itself become an object of market dissemination and commodification for profit while simultaneously being undermined elsewhere.

These economic changes are underpinned by a technological transformation the likes of which the world has never before seen. Gutenberg's revolution has only just begun. Facebook, Instagram, Reddit, and of course Twitter, transform the capacity of billions to communicate with great speed and efficiency. But more importantly, it also transforms the way in which we communicate. As Marshall McLuhan long ago put it, the "medium is the message." These new communication media speed up discourse while flattening it. While a literary culture concerned with books enabled deep consideration of complex ideas, digital culture disseminates information much faster but flattens its substantive content into bite-sized rhetoric or ironic cynicism. The consequence has been a movement towards "one dimensional" communication. This is coupled with the rise of entertainment technologies which allow us to increasingly "amuse ourselves to death" to use Neil Postman's unforgettable phrase. Radio and television were the forerunners of post-modern culture, compressing complex topics down into ever shorter bursts of informational overload competing for listeners and viewers in an ever more media saturated culture. Now, with the emergence of the internet, YouTube, blogs, and online fake universities we have access to more information, true and false, than ever before. One of the negative consequences of these developments has been a competition for attention by upping the rhetorical ante while downplaying substance. We have resultantly seen a strange increase in hyper-partisanship and mean-spiritedness in many post-modern media. This in turn has an impact on politics, as liberal concerns about the greater good gives way to a competition for attention and one upmanship, resulting in a political culture of "ownage" that more closely resembles a wrestling match presided over by the Donald than a traditional democratic polity organized by "ordered liberty" and communitarian resemblance.

The End of Conservatism

The paradox of post-modern culture is that as information flattens and communication becomes more one dimensional, economic interconnectedness and technological transformation speeds up. As Paul Virilio puts it, post-modern culture is nothing if not one of "speed." This makes traditionalist conservatism increasingly untenable as a political ideology. The flattening of discourse and communication, combined with the availability of so many forms of entertainment and spectacle, eradicates the necessary conditions for integrating into any consistent culture in any depth over an extended period of time. Economic "creative destruction" eradicates traditionalist barriers to the creation of new values that can be used to market new commodities. Even religion itself becomes a marketable product which can in turn become an object of competition in the so called "culture war." These trends in post-modern culture demonstrate the limitations of conservative traditionalism to deal with what has been happening. Roger Scruton decries the emergence of Trump and Trumpism as symptomatic of the "decline" of culture, while never sufficiently interrogating those forces-including capitalist markets-that help bring it about.

The end of conservatism doesn't mean the end of reactionary ideologies. What Trump and Trumpism embodies is what I have elsewhere called "post-modern conservatism." Post-modern conservatism is a form of identity politics that emerges as a reaction against post-modern culture, while remaining very much its product. It mobilizes the anxieties produced by constant economic and technological transformations, often using hyper-real mediums such as the internet and hyper-partisan news agencies to rally political attention and stoke resentment. It then directs these energies against perceived enemies who are allegedly responsible for these undesirable transformations, often alleged foreigners and their allies in the thoroughly modernist "literary" cultures of academia and the traditional print media, and uses their presence to justify seizing state power and cracking down on change. Of course, the solutions offered and the tactics deployed by post-modern conservatism are invariably symptomatic of post-modern culture. This means that in many ways they only exacerbate the initial anxieties, leading to a vicious cycle of ever increasing partisanship and reactionary paranoia.

It is uncertain whether post-modern conservatism will become the conservatism of the 21st century, or whether new variations will emerge which may be preferable. But it seems clear to me that, as the social forces underpinning post-modern culture pick up speed, the traditionalist conservatism mourned by Scruton, Deneen, and others has likely met its end. What is unclear to me is whether this is a good thing.

Right Wing Critiques of Identity Politics and Post-Modern Culture

Matt McManus

Introduction

In his intellectual blockbuster *Why Liberalism Failed,* Patrick Deneen makes a powerful argument for why liberalism-despite being the only surviving political ideology with moral currency after the long 20th century- has been ridden by internal ideological and practical tensions since its inception. For instance, while promoting the moral equality of all, the economic doctrines affiliated with liberalism have led to widening material inequality and resultant social instability. It draws on contractarian and democratic doctrines to legitimate liberal political systems, while simultaneously emphasizing the individual and their private pursuits over civic involvement. As a result of these, and other tensions, Deneen observes that it is no great surprise that liberalism is rapidly losing moral currency despite not facing an existentially threatening external enemy. He believes that the emergence of right wing and left wing identity oriented movements, and the authoritarian slant which characterizes many of them, is the inevitable consequence of liberalism's internal logic being consistently applied.

Many of Deneen's criticisms echo longstanding critiques by intelligent conservatives about the fundamental tensions embedded at the heart of liberal doctrines. I am going to highlight a very prominent one-the tension of establishing a moral system while distinguishing between means and ends. Following Macintyre, I believe this leads to very serious problems in liberal societies. When compounded by other socio-economic and technological trends, it is responsible for the emergence of a post-modern culture defined by identity politics and the dismissal of "truth" on both the left, and more controversially, the right. I believe we can learn much from these conservative critiques of post-modernity, but we also need to recognize their consistent limitations and seek to go beyond them.

The Means-Ends Distinction

One of Deneen's clear intellectual influences is Alasdair Macintyre, whose great book *After Virtue* was a watershed moment in the history of political theory. In *After Virtue* and other works, Macintyre primarily engages in a complex rediscovery and rearticulation of "virtue ethics," drawing primarily on Aristotle (the master of those who know, after all). While engaging and inspiring, I will not discuss this dimension of Macintyre's thought extensively here. Instead I wish to briefly summarize his account of modernity and the challenges facing modern liberalism, before discussing why I think Macintyre can help us understand the emergence of post-modern culture.

Macintyre makes many significant criticisms of liberal doctrines, but the most integral is liberalism's distinction between "means" and "ends." He clarifies this distinction by juxtaposing modern with Ancient (Greek) morality. In the Greek world, the goal of morality was pursuing the highest end of human perfection and happiness, what Aristotle termed Eudaimonia. Eudaimonia was not achieved by simply pursuing one's private pleasure. Instead it was achieved by developing established excellent qualities-virtues-which enabled one to become an increasingly honored member of one's community. Achieving Eudaimonia was an art one needed to improve upon throughout life as it was the end or *telos* of our human existence.

Macintyre juxtaposes this against the modern liberal argument that the locus of morality is not teleological, but formal. In the early liberals, the point of life becomes not the telos of Eudaimonia, but the private pursuit of pleasures and material happiness. What matters for morality then becomes exclusively about the means to achieve happiness for all, rather than the ends which we are all supposed to pursue. The theoretical consequence of this according to Macintyre is that it leads to meta-ethical emotivism; the idea that what is right and wrong is purely a matter of taste and opinion. What is "moral" for one person, such as the pursuit of riches through the production of pornography, might not be moral for another person who might choose to work for a charity. According to Macintyre, liberalism has no way of determining which of these pursuits is more "moral" than the other since it is left to individuals to decide which ends are important to them. Culturally, in the long run this leads to a nihilistic society where individuals are disconnected from and indifferent to one another. They exist as atomized selves whose only abiding moral concern is that their "rights" to pursue pleasure are fully respected by others. Macintyre does not believe such a culture can persist in the long run. As he put it in the apocalyptic final passages of *After Virtue:*

"A crucial turning point in that earlier history occurred when men and women of good will turned aside from the task of shoring up the Roman imperium and ceased to identify the continuation of civility and moral community with the maintenance of that imperium. What they set themselves to achieve instead . . . was the construction of new forms of community within which the moral life could be sustained so that both morality and civility might survive the coming ages of barbarism and darkness. If my account of our moral condition is correct, we ought also to conclude that for some time now we too have reached that turning point. . . . This time however, the barbarians are not waiting beyond the frontiers; they have already been governing us for quite some time. And it is our lack of consciousness of this that constitutes part of our predicament. We are waiting not for a Godot, but for another—doubtless quite different—St. Benedict."

These beliefs are echoed by Deneen in *Why Liberalism*

Failed. He does not believe that liberalism has failed due to a crisis of faith, or from being misapplied. Instead it emerged because liberalism is unable to resolve its fundamental tensions. The most notable of these is related in a very key way to the Macintyrean claim about the means-ends distinction. According to Deneen, liberalism creates a society where individuals feel they should be free to pursue any objectives in life without being subject to moral limitations. But we then come to realize that we are still faced with inescapable physical and social limitations which inhibit the pursuit of our desire; including our desire to inhabit a given identity that might be different from that which is ascribed to us. According to Deneen, this leads to a growing demand to use the state to efface these perceived limitations on the realization of our inner identity and its desires.

Post-Modern Culture

In our increasingly anxious political environment it is hard not to sympathize with Macintyre and Deneen's assessment. But where I think Macintyre and Deneen don't go far enough is in looking at the social factors which contribute to the emergence of nihilistic post-modern culture. They tend to brilliantly explore the influence of intellectual ideas and their formulation as idealized ideologies, which is undeniably a crucial task in understanding how we got where we are. But we also need to look at other factors as well. There are key limitations to these claims . Macintyre and Deneen both fall victim to a characteristic weakness in many (but not all!) conservative critiques of post-modernity: their arguments tend to operate at a very abstract level which does not take into account complex material and technological transformations at play in society. This is because their critiques are primarily moral in nature, which in turn has the consequence of individuating blame for destructive social trends on given people or cultures. This is inadequate for understanding how we have gotten where we are.

Contemporary society is indeed one where the claim that there are no obvious ends to which we should all strive is taken for granted. But liberalism as a doctrine, and liberal political systems are not the only culprits here. I believe that both socio-economic and technological transformations also play a substantial role. This is where left critiques of post-modernity have always had the edge on their conservative counterparts, and given the emergence of new forms of right wing post-modern authoritarianism, the need for them has rarely been greater.

The neo-liberal economic system we live within is predicated on rampant consumerism and the satisfaction of private desire. It cannot function consistently unless individuals feel their primary aim in life should be the pursuit of commodities. Whether this be a private and isolated homestead located far from everyone else, or the latest electronic device enabling one to spend ever greater time in digital communication bubbles cut off from the broader culture. Moreover, neoliberal economic imperatives don't simply direct firms to satisfy the already existent desires of others. As was well established by Max Weber, Joseph Schumpeter and others, firms are also very active in the creation of new desires through the development of novel products, the immense sums spent on marketing, attracting social capital to commodities and so on. While engaging in these processes of "creative-destruction" economic firms overturn traditional and personalized ways of living and interacting, particularly those moral, legal, and political barriers which prevent them from marketing and selling new products. This leads to ever greater social fragmentation through the dissolution of old values and institutions. This is often justified by appealing to the liberal "right" of consumers to acquire what they want-or more accurately-what they were driven to want by firms. While by no means common in contemporary right wing discourse, some sharper conservative critiques have noted this tendency, though their analysis of it tends to fall short of what is needed. As put by Deneen in his 2015 essay "The Power Elite" discussing the Indiana RFRA law:

"Corporations exist to make money, not to advance political and social causes—except for those that help them make money, of course. And that's just the point: the decision by Apple, Walmart, Eli Lilly, Angie's List, and so on was a business decision—even more, a marketing decision. Coming out in opposition to the Indiana RFRA law was one of the shrewdest marketing coups since E.T. followed a trail of Reese's Pieces. The decision to #BoycottIndiana was not made because it was the politically courageous thing to do; it was made because it was the profitable thing to do. The establishment could express support for a fashionable social norm while exerting very little effort, incurring no actual cost, and making no sacrifice to secure the goal."

The social fragmentation produced by these socio-economic trends is compounded immensely by additional economic insecurities. As professions rise and fall, jobs are shipped overseas, and inequality soars, it leads to a growing number of people witnessing the very material facts of their existence change with unparalleled rapidity. This leads to a great deal of anxiety, both about change in itself and its material consequences for individuals and their families.

These socio-economic trends are coupled with developments in modern technology and technological culture. These are particularly driven by digital and communications technologies. The internet has tremendous potential to enable individuals to communicate with countless others around the globe. Under better circumstances that might lead to the virtues of a more informed civic dialogue and a better understanding of what one's ideological opponents are saying. Unfortunately that is rarely what happens. In these hyper-real mediums, individuals deal with the anomie produced by modern economic and social transformations by turning to others on the internet who feel very much like they do . Driven by resentment, they come to feel that their happiness and identity is under attack by mysterious antagonists which are often not well defined; a factor which contributes to their perceived omnipresence. Because these individuals operate in a moral culture where the pursuit of one's private happiness is taken as the primary focus of life, they react to these perceived wrongs in a highly antagonistic and even paranoid fashion.

One of the results of all these factors is the emergence of today's identity politics on the left and the right. Identity politics is the product of a post-modern culture where the liberal dismissal of ends, and the consequent economic and technological transformations that align with it, combine to produce angry and resentful populations. These populations align with others who affiliate with given group identities to push for the political power needed to better pursue their collective desires.

Post-Modern Conservatism? Yes It's a Thing (A Reply to Andrew Urban)

Matt McManus

In July 2018 Andrew Urban published an article "A quick quiz you can't win" responding to my essay "What is a Post-Modern Conservative?" (republished as the preface to this book). The essence of my argument was that post-modernism isn't just a fancy theoretical tradition propagated from the ivory tower downwards, and which encourages a few over-sensitive undergraduate students to demand safe spaces and censor everyone they disagree with. Drawing on other writers like Marshall McLuhan-a fellow Canuck of "global village" fame- and Neil Postman I maintain that post-modernism is a specific culture which has had a dramatic impact on the way many Westerners understand truth, individuality, and political movements. The initial political impact of this post-modern culture was seen on the Left end of the spectrum, with a host of philosophers and commentators developing new theories and the various identity politics we are all too familiar with mobilizing. I then proceeded to claim that post-modern culture was now having an impact on the Right, leading to the emergence of what I call post-modern conservatism. This can be seen with the rise of truth ignoring, identity politics propagating, "alternative-facts"-worshiping-politicians like Donald Trump in the United States and Viktor Orban in Hungary.

Now I did not coin the term "post-modern conservative." That honor belongs to the deceased political theorist (and staunch conservative Catholic) Peter Lawler, who used it as a positive label for what he thought conservatism should become. But I have used the term post-modern conservatism very differently and much more critically, and have published on the topic to try and indicate how many political movements on the Right have gradually evolved into what they claimed to have hated more than anything else. The essay summarized the five main features of what I take a post-modern conservative to be, and why we should be concerned that they have emerged.

Andrew Urban's response to my essay didn't really address any of this. Without context he presented my list of the five features I associated with post-modern conservatism, and then proceeded to mock it for an apparent lack of self-awareness. Now as a Canadian he may have just been using some Aussie humor (though I roomed with an Australian for a long time and figured I had that down). But his quick little article seemed to just presume that I was apparently a Leftist (true enough), which of course means I support post-modern identity politics (not really, it's complicated), and therefore wasn't aware of the irony in my (wrongly???) calling out conservatives for adopting the same positions and practices.

If I've gotten his position right, then Urban's article seems based on quite a few presumptions and inaccuracies. Firstly, it seems to assume that all people on the left end of the political spectrum invariably support post-modernism and identity politics. This is simply untrue. In fact, many of the most vicious attacks on post-modern theory come from left-liberals like Ronald Dworkin and Martha Nussbaum, Marxists like David Harvey and Fredric Jameson, and human-dignity-loving-international-rights-scholars such as myself. The Left isn't one ideological movement, and it is wrong to judge it based on what a few rather vocal activists and theorists say. Secondly, Andrew Urban seems to think my argument is blatantly untrue and therefore doesn't deserve serious consideration. Ironically enough, that kind of hyper-partisan attitude towards reasoned debate is one of the features of post-modern conservatism I provide on my list. If he thinks my argument is wrong, he is welcome to try and explain why. Just having a partisan laugh without actually engaging with what I said is very far from convincing.

Part II

Post-Modern Conservatism and Post-Modern Culture

Politics as Entertainment: Partisanship in Post-Modern Culture

Matt McManus

Introduction

In his seminal *Amusing Ourselves to Death* the sociologist Neil Postman observed that there were two important dystopian novels released in the early 20th century. The first was George Orwell's *1984*. Humankind would be overwhelmed by a trio of totalitarian parties, which would establish a state where secret police, historical revisionism, and abject violence would be omnipresent. The pretext of that novel was that ultimately everything we hate was going to destroy us. The second dystopian masterpiece was Aldous Huxley's *Brave New World.* In it, humankind is overtaken by a benevolent dictatorship which permits rampant use of drugs, sexual liberality, and provides a continuous stream of entertainment. All to keep people distracted, disinterested, and finally unable to even think about the banal authoritarian society in which they lived out interchangeable existences. The pretext of this novel was that ultimately everything we love all too easily was going to destroy us. Postman's warning in *Amusing Ourselves to Death* was that Huxley may well have been right.

Many contemporary authors have commented on the simultaneous emergence of right wing populism-what I have called post-modern conservatism-and linked it to the growth of hyper-partisanship in the media, across the internet, and so on. These trends are quite real and exceptionally dangerous, as the one dimensional partisanship shown by individuals across the political spectrum belies a stultifying incapacity to critically reason through complex material. Instead, difficult and challenging social phenomena are flattened by post-modern technologies and hyper-partisanship into easily digestible narratives and slogans which are imposed upon and propagated by democratic communities transformed into what Theodor Adorno called the "masses." This transition of potentially critically minded democratic communities into masses is the result of a long historical process which included economic, social, and technological transformations of immense significance. Here, I will discuss the last of these to try and showcase how politics in post-modern culture evolved into a form of entertainment, depleting the ability of individuals to critically evaluate facts and norms about political issues.

The Culture Industry and the Rise of New Media

Post-modernism is best understood along two interrelated lines. The first is as an umbrella term applying to a movement in the Western theoretical tradition. Thinkers such as Jacques Derrida and Michel Foucault posed significant philosophical and linguistic challenges to the claim that human beings could recognize how the world operated with any kind of objective certainty. The second is as an epoch-of a culture-in the history of Western civilization. It is this second interpretation which I find more convincing, and is what I will be discussing here.

Post-modern culture is defined in part by the surge of media, entertainment, and communications technologies which have emerged in the past century. The speed with which these transformations take place, and the deliberately immediate and easy way in which we incorporate these new technologies into our daily life, can distract from the impact such changes have. We have come a very long way since Johannes Gutenberg first printed the Bible in the 1450s. Many now experience a daily existence where they are saturated with information provided by the media and through digital communications, and can readily access a virtually infinite library on the internet.

There are two temptations that must be avoided when

understanding this phenomenon in post-modern culture. The first is to refrain from thinking that the way we digest information is the same as it ever was; the only difference is that we have access to a great deal more of it. As Marshall McLuhan rightly put it, we must recognize that the "medium is the message." These post-modern technologies do enable us to better access information. But they also establish a culture where we are so bombarded with it, that there is a constant competition for our attention and concern. This transforms the way in which information is presented. What McLuhan and Postman would call literary or print cultures or societies, where information is presented as long form texts and speeches with ample space and time to present nuance and complexity, gives way to a flattened digital society within the broader post-modern culture. Information is presented in as accessible *and entertaining* a way as possible. This also has consequences for how politics operates.

In *Amusing Ourselves to Death* Postman observes that television had a transformative effect on politics in the United States. Television encouraged politicians to concern themselves more with the optics of presentation and style than the substance of what they were saying. It also forced them to increasingly compress discussions and observations about massively complicated policy choices into flattened sound bites and slogans that could be readily presented and remembered in 5 minutes on networks like CNN and Fox. This need to be "catchy" also compelled politicians to further favor being entertaining and memorable over providing substantive information and engaging in genuine debate. And, he warned, this was simply the effect of "new" technologies such as radio and television. One can only imagine what he would think in this new world of Twitter, where the President of the United States summarizes the state of the union in a few hundred characters and plenty of hyperbole!!!

Postman follows other great critical theorists such as Theodor

Adorno in warning that this flattening of communication, and the tendency to favor entertainment over substance, was having a debilitating effect on society. These new technologies gradually weaned of us of our capacity and interest in engaging in serious and rational critical analysis. As literary cultures give way to flattened post-modern culture, we lose our ability to apply concerted analytical attention to complex issues, instead favoring easily digestible entertainment and immediate affect. The impact of this on politics is to make individuals increasingly attracted to those who offer easy solutions to complex problems, and who can combine political agitation with the entertainment usually associated with spectacle.

These problems are compounded by the fact that many people are not encouraged to use new technologies to broaden their intellectual horizons. Facebook, Twitter, YouTube and many other new media deploy complex algorithms to ensure that individuals are exposed to an endless circuit of information proffering the same ideological biases. The result is paradoxical: individuals with access to more information than ever before are also increasingly closed off from new sources of information and ideological disagreement. They operate within what is often called "communication bubbles": continuously interacting with the same types of individuals and imbibing the same ideological material over and over again. This has the function of transforming them from critically minded individual citizens in a democratic polity into what Adorno called the "masses"-a collectivity concerned with simultaneously seeking out authority and power in another, while wanting to exercise it against those too weak to resist.

Conclusion: Politics as Entertainment and Postmodern Culture

Hyper-partisanship thrives in such a post-modern technological environment. The spectacle of partisanship draws attention and provides distraction for individuals already enclosed within limited communication bubbles propagating the same ideological talking points. Political positions calcify as individuals are offered endless opportunity to feel outrage and express long repressed forces of aggression against ideological opponents whom one need never see or dialogue with; something which pundits like Stefan Molyneux and Ezra Levant are giddy to exploit for profit. The atmosphere starts to more closely approximate a sports match, with an endless series of memes and videos discussing how a "Feminist was OWNED" or a "SNOWFLAKE SJW WAS CUCKED." The endlessly aggressive and emotional rhetoric belies the growing lack of substance behind any of these perceived victories. Ironically, the manufactured demand for hyper-partisan spectacle also engenders a greater sense of victimization and resentment. Since the point of politics increasingly becomes to achieve victory over one's opponents, and not to enact any sincere agenda, the enemy must always return to be destroyed yet again. This demonstrates what Hannah Arendt would characterize as the "impotent bigness" of so many of these hyper-partisan figures reorienting politics as a kind of entertainment. Their endlessly bombastic rhetoric and appeal to "mass" culture belies the weakness and paranoia underpinning their constant need to seek affirmation in the destruction and subsequent resurrection of their political opponents.

No one embodies the new form of politics and entertainment-and therefore the politics of post-modern culture as a whole-better than Donald Trump; a man who literally presided over the "Battle of the Billionaires" wrestling match. Trump himself is the embodiment of what Adorno would call the "great little man"-"a person who suggests both omnipotence and the idea that he is just one of the folks, a plain red-blooded American untainted by material or spiritual wealth." His narcissistic demands for attention and power, gutted of any substance, are immensely attractive to an audience weaned in post-modern culture and who seek distraction from its many ambiguities and disappointments. Trump has not disappointed, delivering a political climate flush with take downs, vulgarity, a hyper-partisan disdain for the truth, and a love of combative identity politics where one's team is always in combat with another. He should be interpreted as what he is: a sad and impotent symptom of our post-modern culture who must be understood before he can be defeated.

Trump and the Age of Bullshit- The Roots of a Knowledge Crisis

Matt McManus

Introduction

By now the claim that Donald Trump is a liar might seem like old news. Well known fact-checker *Politifact* ranked 68 per cent of Trump's statements as veering between "mostly false" to "pants on fire" blatant untruths. This might make it seem like Trump is just any other politician on steroids. It is now broadly accepted that politicians often mislead or lie, which would suggest this is just a worse form of business as usual. But I want to suggest that this is not the case now. Trump is not simply a politician who lies even more than the average person in public office. He is someone who has no conception of truth or falsity whatsoever. What is worse, he has gradually convinced many of his supporters to adopt this dismissive approach to knowledge and truth. In other words Trump is heralding an age of bullshit.

Truth and Bullshit

To think through what this new age brings, it is helpful to look a little at the literature on the subject. The classic work on the subject is Professor of Philosophy Harry Frankfurt's 2005 opus *On Bullshit.* Frankfurt argues that there is a distinction between being a liar and telling lies, and being a bullshitter. A liar, such as President Nixon, still fundamentally accepts that there is a difference between telling the truth and telling a lie. Indeed, they spend a great deal of their time trying to conceal their falsehoods because they acknowledge that what they said doesn't correspond to objective reality. By contrast, a bullshitter doesn't care or doesn't understand the difference between truth and falsehood. To them, reality is what one makes of it; or worse, what one wants it to be. When a bullshitter speaks, it is with indifference or even hostility to the whole concept that there might be a real world out there which can and will contradict their statements.

Now consider Donald Trump. In *The Art of the Deal,* Trump acknowledged that he didn't think that misleading people or himself was a fundamental wrong:

"People want to believe that something is the biggest and the greatest and the most spectacular. I call it truthful hyperbole. It's an innocent form of exaggeration—and a very effective form of promotion."

"Truthful hyperbole" is a colorful way of saying "bullshit your way to success if you have to." It doesn't matter as long as you get to the top, since people want to believe in exaggerated and self-glorifying stories that make themselves feel better. And that has been the philosophy guiding Trump's presidency. When confronted by the fact that he lost the popular vote to Hilary Clinton and had lied about it by blaming non-existent illegal voters, Trump countered that it didn't matter since so many people believed him. When it became obvious that his inauguration crowd was smaller than Obama's, he rejected what his eyes told him and appealed to "alternative facts." When commentators pointed out that the US imposes tariffs on all kinds of goods, he played the victim and started a trade war anyway. And the list goes on.

Conclusion

What we see here are not simply lies told by a serial liar. It is someone who is indifferent to, or incapable of recognizing, the very idea of truth. And to my mind that is the most dangerous long term legacy of Trump. He is inaugurating an Age where what is real or what is false should have no bearing on policy decisions, or rectifying trade imbalances, or maintaining relations with allies. What matters is that Trump's simultaneously self-pitying and aggrandizing spin makes his supporters feel better. He's playing to their contradictory desire for greatness and feelings of being victimized by cultural and media "elites" who bring out their facts and tables insisting Trump and his supporters are just wrong. And Trump's postmodern conservatism is winning. As his Presidency carries on it becomes increasingly difficult for people to know what is real or false, or even to care about the difference. It is frightening to guess at what this aversion to reality might lead the most powerful man in the world to do.

Benjamin, Aesthetics and the Political Practices of the Alt Right

Matt McManus and Erik Tate

The Work of Art in the Age of Mechanical Reproduction

German-Jewish literary and cultural critic Walter Benjamin was one of the great analysts of liberal capitalism during the interwar period when capitalism's flaws seemed to be materializing and fascism had become an alternate form of political organization that was ascendant across Europe. To many, the capitalist mode of production seemed on the verge of extinction and alternatives had to be sought out. Benjamin searched for these alternatives with reference to art and the new meanings the concept of art had taken on since the emergence of photography and, subsequently, film. Much of his work is concerned with the relation of cultural products and social processes characteristic of a civilization to inner psychic and spiritual tensions roiling beneath the surface of hegemonic ideologies.

Written in multiple versions during the late 1930s with the first completed in 1936, "The Work of Art in the Age of Mechanical Reproduction" is primarily concerned with the historical development of art. In this essay, Benjamin also continues his effort to articulate the revolutionary potential that he sees in contemporary art forms as he discusses the implications that emerging technologies have for the function of art in modern society. In order to do so, Benjamin links large-scale forms of collective organization to the mode of perception that characterizes them, that is, the dominant medium through which the human experience of the world is filtered. The mode of perception is largely determined by the dominant mode of production that underlies a society so, he claims, the way humans experience the world depends on historically shifting media of perception. The historical development of perception can reflect crises and massive social upheavals such as the increasingly evident crisis of the capitalist mode of production.

Benjamin saw that his world had become perceptually organized around film, which requires a different kind of visual literacy than was previously the case. There are 3 overarching points to be made about the new mode of perception. It is the result of the "reproducibility" that the photographic mode of production lends to things; people generally have greater access to artistic production, which is no longer limited to a privileged audience and a special class of craftsmen working under a master; and reception of cultural products is now organized around the distracted masses as opposed to the contemplative individual. Distraction, in other words, emerges from Benjamin's analysis as the way in which we receive cultural products. Benjamin points out that architecture is often received in distraction. We no longer see it once we have integrated it into the course of our daily lives and formed habits and patterns of behavior around it. Photographic reproduction, he argues, lends this quality that architecture has always possessed to the rest of the world because of the three points above. Now art and cultural products in general can be (re)produced and disseminated easily and with incredible rapidity, and the ability of people to participate in the formative processes that determine the way we perceive our shared world is one of the great democratizing potentials that Benjamin saw in this new technologically-administered perceptual mode characterized by what he calls the "decay of the aura."

For the purposes of this paper, however, we will focus largely on the negative side of this development, as Benjamin would have it, and set aside what he saw as its great potential to democratize cultural production. We will do this by focusing on the fact that since art can now be reproduced and spread across the body politic with incredible speed, it has become a powerful tool for the maintenance of power structures, which Benjamin calls "property relations." The maintenance of this relational structure is the primary aim of cultural production turned toward the regressive aims of fascism. It is obviously in the interest of those who have power in society to maintain power or property relations, and, thanks to reproducibility, this can be done by producing and disseminating ideologically loaded aesthetic works which can quickly be deployed as tools of vacuous entertainment or propaganda.

But notably, Benjamin made another and far deeper point at the conclusion of his essay. Noting how the rise of reactionary fascism was in part dependent on the paradoxical use of the most powerfully modern technologies to deploy propaganda, he pondered what this said about the subjects of fascist regimes. His conclusion was quite striking. The capacity of modern societies to reproduce artistic materials had become so pronounced that in fascist countries it had produced a very new type of social organization. If Marx once predicted that the melting into air of all that is solid would progress to the point where "man is at last compelled to face with sober senses his real conditions of life, and relations with his kind," Benjamin is now predicting that under this new form of fascist organization, society could potentially become so self-alienated and detached from worldly concerns that "it can experience its own annihilation as a supreme aesthetic pleasure." Fascism is essentially a society that has transformed itself into a rigid hierarchy that pacifies its subjects through vacuous entertainment and meaningless forms of expression - politics is reduced to an aesthetic spectacle. The alienated masses of people are allowed everything short of actually curbing the insidious forces of exploitation that continue to efface their individuality. As he puts it in the Epilogue:

"The increasing proletarianization of modern man and the increasing formation of masses are two aspects of the same process. Fascism attempts to organize the newly proletarianized masses while leaving intact the property relations which they strive to abolish. It sees its salvation in granting expression to the masses – but on no account granting them their rights. The masses have a *right* to changed property relations; Fascism seeks to give them *expression* in keeping these relations unchanged. *The logical outcome of Fascism is an aestheticizing of political life."*

Benjamin's essay was written after 1935 as cinema was just cresting in its cultural influence. Films such as *Triumph of the Will* overtly deployed technology to produce a new aestheticization of politics, most of which reached a pitch in the call for war and violence. He compares such works to Marinetti's futurist manifesto, which glorifies war and its handmaiden, industry. Anticipating Stanley Kubrick's black comedy *Dr. Strangelove* many years in the future, Benjamin suggests that we would plunge so far into war and alienation of our darkest impulses that even acts of wanton destruction and annihilation would increasingly be regarded as acceptable because they drew people out of themselves for a brief period of time. The connection between such an aesthetics and support for an increasingly authoritarian and paranoid political culture is not hard to discern. Moreover, as we shall see, it also plays an integral role in the formation of broader historical narratives which must also be analyzed and challenged.

The Aestheticization of Politics and the Alt-Right

Benjamin's endlessly provocative essay is a useful starting point for thinking about the way that the politics of certain sects of the modern right have become fundamentally related to aesthetics. Benjamin is unflinching in his condemnation of using technology to introduce aesthetics into politics: *"All efforts to aestheticize politics culminate in one point. That point is war."* This is because war is the primary way in which society and technology can be mobilized *en masse* while changing nothing about the oppressive organization upon which that society is based. But while Benjamin is a useful place to start, we need to go beyond his analysis. We must examine how what is effectively post-modern conservatism uses the now exponentially more powerful technological tools of digital media and communications to disseminate its paranoid messages.

The alt right emerged as the product of complex conditions in society, but its first instantiations were online. Individuals felt increasingly alienated in a society which no longer conformed to their expectations, often dealing with disappointment at their inability to live up to the American Dream in a climate of economic decline. Moreover, they came to feel that the triumphalist historical narratives about American supremacy, often affiliated with the ascendency of white protestant norms to the status of universal ideology, were increasingly being challenged. The psychic protection these alienated individuals felt by affiliating with this triumphalist historical narrative about American greatness was undercut by counter narratives about the persistence of past wrongs towards groups like women, African Americans, and the developing world more broadly. These counter narratives were promulgated by seemingly alien groups within society who were simultaneously both all-pervasive and hegemonic, while also not embodying the traits of "real" Americans.

As the historical narratives about American greatness were undercut, and the psychic defense it provided against alienation faded, many in the future alt-right turned to distraction to express their resentment. This took the form of a dizzying and growing array of right wing aesthetics whose primary purpose was no longer to present a clear and consistent political ideology. Classical conservatism, while certainly preceding the alt right, was at least concerned for presenting itself as an intellectually consistent system of thought. William F. Buckley's snide pretensions shouldn't distract us from the fact that many took his unique blend of moralistic Protestantism, support for unbridled individualistic capitalism, and robust international interventionism, to be a genuinely plausible worldview. But the alt right was never concerned with that. This is why, despite its apparent hatred of post-modernity, the alt right is very much a post-modern movement. Its relativism and distrust of any "truth" but that which flows from the communications bubble is indicative of the conditions of its birth.

Digital technologies, with their capacity to simultaneously open up new spaces for thought while enabling individuals to increasingly live within a communications bubble, meant that most alt righters never needed to concern themselves with the intellectual salience of their ideology. They could concern themselves increasingly with distraction; the most satisfying of which was often to undermine and stereotype all those they felt were responsible for their sense of alienation. Intellectuals, Women, LGBTQ individuals, Muslims, Democrats, Hollywood celebrities – each was targeted in turn by memes, pod-casts, videos, fake news. This was all designed to present a minimum of intellectual content in the most affective manner possible. In other words it was designed as ideological entertainment which played to the psychic desires of alt-righters to have their resentments stoked.

Of course many of the alt right could not give plausible reasons why these groups were dangerous. The most offered was that these groups were taken as representative of everything that was holding back "real" Americans; an idealization drawn from stereotypes and clichés that never had much basis in reality. But that is what Benjamin taught us long ago, and what is more clearly important than ever before. The aestheticization of politics is designed to give the masses an outlet for their anger and resentment without actually addressing the underlying issues in a meaningful way. For Benjamin these issues boil down to the essentially fascist goal of propagating an exploitative and crushingly hierarchical set of property relations. New technologies are embraced by fascism precisely because they allow these vitriolic feelings to be expressed so that they can be used as an excuse for furthering an agenda of authoritarian domestic policies at home and engaging in interventionist wars abroad – all of this without allowing the critical evaluation of power relations, much less the direct access of the masses to political life. Just as entertainment without critical engagement amounts to incapacitation, the entry of aesthetics into politics actually has the effect of *anaesthetizing* the masses. One can express one's resentment or disenchantment easily enough, but the trick of a "postmodernized" right is to allow this expression but deny the masses their right to actually influence power or property relations. But once one steps beyond mere expression, the greater historical problems of an aestheticized politics become clear.

The aesthetic tools of postmodern conservatism do more than just provide an apolitical outlet for the resentments of the alienated. Though this is their day to day function, they serve another purpose. They allow the alt-right the opportunity to reconstruct an account of history which superficially redeems and resurrects the formerly triumphalist narrative. "Make America Great Again" is a call to return to a triumphalist narrative by ridding the state of those whose mere presence increasingly challenges it by serving as a reminder of American sins past and present. This also demonstrates the fundamental impotence of the alt-right, what Hannah Arendt might have called its "impotent bigness." It wishes to redeem a triumphalist historical narrative by removing those who threaten its credibility. But removing and attacking those same people only serves to reinforce their point about American shame. Few things demonstrate this better than the very election of Donald Trump; sending a trust fund sex-offender to the White House to stick it to those progressives who say rich white men tend to get ahead.

Conclusion

I will conclude by looking at another dimension of Benjamin's work; that concerned with history as a whole and its potential redemption. In his "Theses on the Philosophy of History," Benjamin innovatively pushed against the idea of historical progress while distancing himself from the prognostications of classical Marxism from Marx to Lenin. He pits theology against historical materialism in a reversible Hegelian relation of master-slave by characterizing them as dwarf and puppet, respectively. Unlike liberal narratives which parroted the inevitable triumph of world-wide capitalism, and even their Marxist counterparts who remained firmly committed to the utopian belief in the communist society to come, Benjamin presents us with a far more pessimistic image of the past as a chaos yet to be redeemed.

"There is a painting by Klee called Angelus Novus. An angel is depicted there who looks as though he were about to distance himself from something which he is staring at. His eyes are opened wide, his mouth stands open and his wings are outstretched. The Angel of History must look just so. His face is turned towards the past. Where *we* see the appearance of a chain of events, *he* sees one single catastrophe, which unceasingly piles rubble on top of rubble and hurls it before his feet. He would like to pause for a moment so, to awaken the dead and to piece together what has been smashed. But a storm is blowing from Paradise, it has caught itself up in his wings and is so strong that the Angel can no longer close them. The storm drives him irresistibly into the future, to which his back is turned, while the rubble-heap before him grows sky-high. That which we call progress, is *this* storm."

Here Benjamin's condensed and imagistic thinking comes out in full force. This allegorical reading of Klee's painting presents history not as a string of moments like beads on a string, but as a heap of refuse still piling up from that originary catastrophe, that fall from divinity. The angel is looking at the viewer, implying that it is us who are the rubble of this catastrophe. For the divine to reemerge in the context of history, for what was smashed to again become whole, is the focal point of Benjamin's historicism, the possibility of which seems always suspended or deferred. The first step, however, is to turn away, to try and see as the angel of history sees and refigure history in the way that Benjamin is trying to show us, to not look "forward" at progress or utopia but rather backward toward the past in order to prophesy the *present*.

Benjamin's solution to the problem of historical progress as chaos is messianic; we can only redeem the broken history of the past by effacing its alienation in the present. Just as the masses have a *right* to changed property relations that is yet to be realized, so too does the past maintain a claim to redemption in the now. In recognizing history in this way, we establish a present in which "splinters of messianic time" are shot through. Accomplishing this means turning people from an aestheticized politics in which history is always written by the victor, to borrow Nietzsche's formulation, toward the oppressed past, which would constitute a confrontation with the real sources of alienation and the complex histories underpinning them. Benjamin's revisionary materialism, in a move characteristic of his thinking, calls for reversal, not an aestheticized politics but a politicized aesthetics – aesthetics he links to its Greek origin as perception and a theory of experiencing the world.

Benjamin's image of history presents a model for this reversal because it is just that, an image, a dialectical movement brought to a standstill. History is handed down as tradition, but in the handing down it is also destroyed. If we stop and piece it back together, as the angel would like to do, history keeps happening. Redemption is only possible through messianic intervention. Yet again, however, Benjamin resists prognostication in a way that is echoed in Kafka's formulation of hope: "There is hope – only not for us." Redemption is the future, only not *our* future. This is because reading the "text" of history – like the destruction of a sample in order to analyze it in the lab – is also a destructive act, effacing those voices that demand recognition, those specters that haunt our present with their unfinished business. We can start to acknowledge a renewed sense of history by demonstrating that as long as the alt right attempts to redeem a false narrative of American greatness through embodying the most ugly characteristics found in America's history, it is doomed to impotent failure.

Carl Schmitt, Liberalism, and Post-Modern Conservatism

Matt McManus

Introduction

In the post-modern epoch's climate of political partisanship, many are debating what constitutes legitimate political disagreement and rational discourse about politics. Liberals and their defendants are increasingly pressed by post-modernist movements from the left, and as we shall see, on the right, who do not hold to traditional liberal values about the importance of free speech and inquiry. Most liberal thinkers blame their opponents for these tendencies. I think it is important to evaluate whether this is true or not, or whether recent trends demonstrate a more fundamental problem within liberalism itself. Here the work of Carl Schmitt can be exceptionally helpful. Here, I discuss how Schmitt can help us understand why and how right wing quasi-authoritarians invoking identity have been able to seize power in liberal states.

Schmitt was a Nazi theorist who was exceptionally critical of social difference, had a lifelong distrust of Marxism and other trends in egalitarian thought, and expressed consistent anti-Semitic and pro-German sentiments. Yet his work has enjoyed an explosion of interest with everyone from political moderates like Jürgen Habermas to more radical thinkers such as Giorgio Agamben and Slavoj Zizek offering commentary on his work. Indeed, some thinkers like Agamben have even formulated their entire theoretical project in relation to Schmitt. This demonstrates the need to have a more comprehensive understanding of his work to see why it remains intriguing to so many left wing theorists who seem like they should be naturally repelled by it.

I think the reason Schmitt's thought remains attractive is

complex. Part of it can be explained by his dramatic and powerful stylistic gifts. Outside of Nietzsche, few German thinkers have established so many provocative and imagistic statements. Another reason for the attraction is Schmitt's ongoing use as foil for thinkers, Habermas most notably, who wish to construct competing theories which avoid Schmittian-type dilemmas. But I think the core of his appeal lies in Schmitt's very powerful criticisms of liberalism and liberal democracy. More than any other thinker, Schmitt challenges the liberal claim to respect difference through the establishment of a tolerant legal regime that enables individuals to live as they please. Given the recent nationalist crackdowns on difference in many purportedly liberal countries, in many ways his work appears more salient than ever before. But we need to reinterpret this in a new way; as the emergence of what I call post-modern conservatism.

Schmitt's Critique of Liberalism

Schmitt was born in 1888 into a conservative Catholic family in the German Empire. While he abandoned his personal religious convictions in the 1920s, the existential and theological contours of his prior faith always colors his work. Schmitt graduated from Strasbourg in 1916 with a thesis on the relationship between the individual and the state, and later held a number of university appointments in law throughout the 1920s and early 1930s. During this time he produced most of the seminal works for which he remains known, including *Political Theology, The Concept of the Political, The Crisis of Parliamentary Democracy,* and his dense magnum opus *Constitutional Theory.* These writings were deeply inspired by the shaky legal and political dynamics of the Weimar Republic, which infamously struggled to contain radical and anti-democratic political parties within a liberal democratic framework. When the Nazi Party took power in 1933, Schmitt served in a number of appointments before the SS eventually forced him to resign due to his alleged "Catholicism" and Hegelianism. After the war, Schmitt lived until 1985 and continued to publish important works including *The Nomos of the Earth* and *The Theory of the Partisan.*

Schmitt's philosophical outlook can be nicely understood as power is never innocent because power is always determinative and decisionist. One of the things he disdained about liberal democracy was its belief that a given legal order could be established which left people free to live their lives as they wished without state interference or control. This belief can still be seen in the work of seminal liberal theorists such as John Rawls and Martha Nussbaum, who remain committed to the idea of a "political" rather than "metaphysical" liberalism which can be legally and politically endorsed by individuals from a wide variety of philosophical perspectives. Such arguments made belief in "liberal pluralism" and multi-culturalism possible.

To Schmitt these liberal pretensions were nonsensical for two reasons. Firstly, Schmitt thought that liberalism's claim to truly respect difference was a sham. This reason is fundamentally related to Schmitt's more general account of how law and politics operates in both liberal and illiberal regimes. For Schmitt, ideologically speaking, all politics is based on incompatible secularized theological concepts. In practice this means that the fundamental concept of the political is the friend/enemy distinction. Political friends are those who conform to our own political theologies, and who wish to see a state and a legal order which conforms to our own outlook. Political enemies are those who hold to a different political theology which is incompatible with our own. The practice of politics is always a form of violence, whether literal or figurative, as different groups of friends and enemies attempt to overcome one another and seize control of the state.

Liberal democracies attempt to quiet politics through the operation of parliamentary democracy. They believe that by giving different groups of friends and enemies space in which

Paranoia and the Post-Modern Right

Dylan DeJong and Matt McManus

Introduction

In contrast to the optimistic rhetoric and optics of neoliberal politicians such as Bill Clinton and Emmanuel Macron, the post-modern right is defined by paranoia. This paranoia is remarkably consistent across the board, and directed against by a loose alliance of elites, the mainstream press, and immigrants bent on destroying national identity.

In March 2018, Hungarian Prime Minister Viktor Orban ominously declared that Europe was "under invasion" by immigrants and warned that "countries that don't stop immigration will be lost." Orban peddles the theory that American-Hungarian magnate George Soros is conspiring with the UN to open Hungary's borders to immigrants. Marine Le Pen, reading the same playbook, proposed to "expel foreigners who preach hatred on our soil" and positioned herself as the sole candidate brave enough to stand against "la caste;" some admixture of pro-EU political elites and the press. Finally, in another hemisphere, we see the hyperbolic, anti-immigration rhetoric of Donald Trump, whose Twitter feed continues to spew invective against the alliance of his political opponents, the news media, and his own justice department. *Why* this post-modern conservatism is characterized by this paranoid rhetoric is a crucial question for progressive thinkers today.

We believe that the paranoia expressed by post-modern conservatives is the symptom of a collective anxiety in an increasingly global society. The paranoia expressed by post-modern conservatives is often directed against nefarious alliances bent on destruction, an ambiguous enemy against which they have no recourse. The character of post-modern right wing paranoia is such that the world of "otherness," which includes everyone from elites to terrorists, are in league with one another to dismantle the paranoiac's world. This is the world of cultural tradition, stability, and order—in short, identity—which must be defended.

The Big Other and the Constitution of Tradition

Here, it is worth looking at the psychoanalytic theories of Jacques Lacan and Slavoj Zizek for guidance. According to these authors, human beings constitute themselves under the gaze of a "big Other." The big Other provides the individual with the standards of behavior which *should* be followed--whether or not the individual agrees. While it does not exist as an actual identity, the big Other is unconsciously accepted as the guarantor of mores and identity. Individuals internalize the rules of the big Other, which give stability to their psychic experience of the world.

Moreover, the mores and traditions we internalize from the big Other link the past to the present, in turn guaranteeing a future which is consistent and stable with what we know. The product of these psychic processes is to construct a consistent, yet highly idealized, worldview. Put more simply, the payoff of adhering to the big Other is a sense of security about how the world is and should be ordered.

There is, however, a tradeoff for acquiring this order and stability. The real world is always more complex and variant than the worldview constructed through these psychic processes. Furthermore, since we are unconsciously aware that our experience of order and security is ultimately constructed, it runs the risk of unraveling; real "otherness" threatens to destroy the world.

Post-modern conservatives succeed by exploiting this haunting anxiety and transforming it into paranoia. They name an external enemy and thus give it coherence—the elite caste, the mainstream media, radicals, and perhaps most unfortunately, immigrants, all of whom form a unified conspiracy to liquidate "us."

On the one hand, the foreign other can be regarded as an invader who must be destroyed. But the root of this fear goes deeper than mere unfamiliarity. The real problem is that the foreign "invader" threatens to reveal that our "big Other," the watchful guarantor of our mores and traditions, is a *local* construction. For example, being confronted with Muslims, who accept the validity of their religion on "faith," threatens to expose the fundamental contingency of the Christian worldview. How can we reject the argument of Muslims who accept the validity of their religion on "faith" and yet maintain that our religious values are unassailably true if they're based on similarly contingent commitments? If we choose not to face such a reality, which would require no less than a reordering of the world itself, the anxious psyche can signify "the Muslim" as an antagonist from which nothing can be learned, and against which "we" must defend ourselves at all costs. The paranoiac worldview of post-modern conservatives is a reactionary defense against all things "other" due to the profound anxiety caused by the possibility that the world might be more complex than their psychic construction.

Establishing the Other as an Enemy

To maintain the coherence of their worldview, post-modern conservatives transform the foreign/cosmopolitan/wealthy "others" into a unified enemy. That enemy, somehow, emerges in their rhetoric as a bizarre alliance of refugees with the global elite, opposing political parties, and cosmopolitan celebrities to advance an agenda, the purpose of which is to infiltrate, steal from, disenfranchise, and terrorize "us." Many liberal critics correctly show that the logic of post-modern conservative positions is contradictory, yet that logic is a symptom rooted in something immune to logic and far more valuable: the coherence of world and one's identity therein.

While we should note the absurdity of blaming both global elites and destitute refugees for the collapse of tradition and order, we also recognize that this confluence is the transference from a real but unidentifiable fear. The paranoiac's world remains stable if Syrian families are the tools through which some powerful cabal plans to undermine society. The paranoiac's world remains stable if Mexican immigrants are a means for the Democratic Party to take and seize power permanently, while the conservative Christian bloc upon which the Republicans depend diminishes in importance due to demographic changes. Post-modern conservatives project the cracks of their worldview's internal conflict, where it fails to be consistent with the real world, to an outward conflict. In this externalized conflict, post-modern conservatives are heroically fighting a war on all fronts. To their peril, rather than adapt their local reality to the changing world, they seek to politically reform the world so that it better resembles the image.

Conclusion

As we have argued elsewhere, the basis of post-modern conservative arguments are not reality, but the hyperreality of a culture war. The conservative postmoderns do not defend Western culture for its merits. Rather, they deride enemies for their part in a cabal seeking their destruction. When analyzed as symptoms of the psychic pressures we have described, it results in an antagonistic politics, vicious in its treatment of both the foreign other and perceived internal enemies. Post-modern conservative paranoia seeks to glaze their inconsistency with hyperreal rhetoric, one which seeks only to preserve the stability of their worldview. Every crack in what they call "our national identity" or "Western civilization" is conveniently covered over, for coming face to face with the other outside is far less taxing than facing the other within.

Politics as a Battle Against Nihilism: Why Conservatives Can't Legislate Past Meaninglessness

Matt McManus

In his 2003 speech to *Civitas,* Stephen Harper, later the Conservative Prime Minister of Canada, made the following comments about the Left's belief systems:

"Conservatives need to reassess our understanding of the modern Left. It has moved beyond old socialistic morality or even moral relativism to something much darker. It has become a moral nihilism – the rejection of any tradition or convention of morality, a post-Marxism with deep resentments, even hatreds, of the norms of free and democratic western civilization. This descent into nihilism should not be surprising because moral relativism simply cannot be sustained as a guiding philosophy."

Since then there has been a veritable explosion of right wing commentary on the dangers of nihilism. Nowhere is this better demonstrated than in Jordan Peterson's sudden rise to fame combating "post-modernism" and "cultural Marxism" which he sees as fundamentally nihilistic forces. They lead to a belief in relativism and meaninglessness, whose consequent demeanors are either both abject cynicism and a rejection of the world, or a totalitarian demand to re-impose order upon it. This is one side of a complex story. The other side is why these post-modern and cultural Marxist philosophies emerged in the first place. For Peterson and others, these philosophies and the movements they inspire are symptoms of a broader movement in Western Civilization away from the inherited traditional values that embody the wisdom of our ancestors. What we therefore need is a return or at least a reevaluation of these traditional values. As Peterson puts it in *12 Rules for Life:An Antidote to Chaos:*

"A long period of unfreedom-adherence to a singular interpretive structure-is necessary for the development of a free mind. Christian dogma provided that unfreedom. But the dogma is dead, at least to the modern Western mind. It perished along with God. What has emerged from behind its corpse, however-and this is an issue of central importance-is something even more dead; something that was never alive, even in the past: nihilism, as well as an equally dangerous susceptibility to new, totalizing, utopian ideas... Nietzsche for his part, posited that individual human beings would have to invent their own values in the aftermath of God's death. But this is the element of his thinking that appears weakest, psychologically: we cannot invent our own values, because we cannot merely impose what we believe on our souls."

Harper and Peterson are just the most articulate and intelligent conservative critics to have made this observation. More comically polemical critics like Dinesh D'Souza, Dennis Prager, and Donald Trump have made similar claims. Ironically, many of the latter group belong to what I have broadly deemed post-modern conservatism: with their identity politics of tradition and authority, and their effacement of truth standards being mobilized in the fights against the alleged boogeymen of nihilistic left wing cultural Marxism.

Here I am going to discuss why so many conservatives seem concerned with the problem of nihilism and what should be done about it. I will make two interrelated claims. The first is that conservatives are correct to be concerned with cultural nihilism, but have misdiagnosed its causes and symptoms. This suggests that moving away from cultural nihilism will take steps which may not be amenable to many modern conservative thinkers. The second claim is that, while we might be able to deal with cultural nihilism, there is no obvious solution to the problem of philosophical nihilism-whether there is an objective answer to the question of life's meaning. Since there is no obvious solution to this problem, we will have to accept that the prospect of philosophical nihilism will remain for a long time to come.

The Conservative Critique of Cultural Nihilism

Cultural nihilism can be broadly understood as the growing social consensus that there are no higher values which society should respect and individuals strive to realize in their own lives. This is often affiliated with the threat of relativism and social fragmentation. Relativism is taken as a symptom of cultural nihilism since if there are no higher values we need to respect and realize, everything is a matter of subjective opinion. There is no standpoint from which we can legitimately criticize or prohibit what others choose to do or value. This in turn leads to social fragmentation. Since there is no standpoint from which to legitimately criticize or prohibit what others choose to do or value, people will increasingly pursue their own private objectives without concern for other individuals or society as a whole. This gradually leads to what Alasdair Macintyre and Charles Taylor termed atomism: the feeling of being alone and valueless-able to do what we want, but without connection or a feeling that what we or anyone else does matters.

Conservative critics like Jordan Peterson date the emergence of cultural nihilism to the origins of modernity. With the Renaissance and then the Enlightenment, came an increasing tendency to question everything. This led to growing skepticism about the wisdom of social conventions, and most importantly, religion itself. This culminated in Nietzsche's legendary proclamation in the 19th century that "God is Dead!" inaugurating a new and nihilistic era in human history. In reaction to the cultural nihilism that emerged with the "death of God," increasingly atomized individuals turned to totalitarianism and cynicism. Early in the 20th century, cultural nihilism is seen as birthing the totalitarian Communist and Nazi movements, which were radical and atheistic attempts to reimpose order on the world. Now that they have disappeared we are witnessing the transformation of individuals into cynical relativists fragmenting society. These cynics developed post-modern cultural Marxist philosophies explicating the implicit doctrines of cultural nihilism.

This explains the almost religious fanaticism with which these conservative critics attack post-modernism. It is not simply a contest of one academic school against another. For critics, like Peterson, this is a battle to rescue the soul of the West from the threat of cultural nihilism. These conservatives argue that we must return to the traditional higher values of the West. Depending on the tenor of the critic, this can either mean returning to classical liberal meritocracy, accepting a kind of cultural Christianity in the case of Peterson, or a full blown return to the churches even if that means accepting irrationalism qua Dostoyevsky.

The Limits of the Conservative Critique of Cultural Nihilism

Cultural nihilism is indeed a dangerous force which should be confronted. The deficiencies of atomism, relativism, and social fragmentation are real and should be confronted by the responsible and concerned. But I do not think conservative critics have adequately diagnosed its causes. Their criticisms mainly operate at a purely ideological level, often in isolation from complex material and technological developments. They look with suspicion at Enlightenment skeptics and outright hostility at post-modern philosophers, seeing them as singularly responsible for the emergence of cultural nihilism. In everyday terms, this often translates into criticizing academics and other "elites" who hold trendy opinions and are apparently singularly responsible for the destruction of society. Firstly, I think this characterization of post-modern thought is deeply flawed and not particularly rigorous. To give just one example, Peterson goes on a long diatribe about Derrida in his latest book and cites not a single work by him. To be blunt, it shows in his poor interpretation of what Derrida actually says. Much the same is true of other conservative critics of "cultural Marxism." But secondly, and far more importantly, it ignores significant forces operating to produce cultural nihilism. This is the deeper problem with conservative criticisms.

Post-modernism was largely a reaction against Marxist "grand narratives" in theory and practice. But the "cultural Marxists" of the Frankfurt School, actually had a great deal to say about cultural nihilism; understandable given that most of them were Jewish emigres fleeing from the Holocaust. They followed Marx's observation that in capitalist society, traditional social values tend to "melt into air." Perhaps more radically given our hyper-partisan times, they also drew on the work of conservative thinkers like Max Weber to radicalize this thesis. They argued that in a capitalist society, people are increasingly driven to see themselves as "one dimensional" beings whose primary focus is satisfying the desires that had been manufactured for them by markets. Capitalism tends to destroy traditional moral barriers to the production of new goods, for instance taboos about sex and responsibility. It also has a dissolving effect on communal relationships, since in capitalist societies individuals were driven to regard themselves and atomized consumers who must "look after themselves" to invoke Margaret Thatcher's memorable phrase. Adorno deepened this concern by observing that in capitalist societies, traditional aesthetic standards of excellence tended to dissolve. The culture industry, concerned to produce easily digestible and primarily entertaining products, avoided the production of artistically challenging and demanding works. Fifty Shades of Grey replaced D.H Lawrence. The total impact of this was to produce a society of atomized and nihilistic consumers quietly consuming to pursue the desires manufactured for them, indifferent to others except when they interfered in the pursuit of this desire.

Later critics have deepened this observation. Alasdair Macintyre has observed that capitalism has had a desultory effect on tradition by encouraging individuals to look only at the means they have-notably money and status-rather than the moral ends they should pursue with others. David Harvey has gone a step further and observed that there is a close affiliation between the latest stage of capitalist society, neoliberalism, and the emergence of post-modern philosophies. He has claimed that post-modernism's focus on "militant particularism"-a fancy word for identity politics-is entirely consistent with the neo-liberal position that individuals should not be constrained in the pursuit of their private and narcissistic sense of identity since many of them will do so primarily through consumption.

Neoliberals also have a concern to destroy moral standards that stand in the way of producing more goods. As Harvey puts it, who do you think is more responsible for the sexualization of culture: a few post-modern professors authoring dense theoretical tracts, or the television industry? Post-modern cultural nihilism is a symptom of cultural change brought about by neo-liberal capitalist practices.

My point here is to observe that conservative critics of cultural nihilism often insulate capitalism and material forces from barbed attacks. This is what attests to their strange and monological focus on universities and academic fads. It is easy enough to attack intellectual elites, who will never inspire the same merit-based respect as a self-made post-modern conservative like Donald Trump. But easy isn't good enough. If cultural nihilism truly is a problem, we need to address it by looking at the far broader and more insidious trends brought about by our social and economic climate.

Conclusion: Nihilism as a Philosophical Problem

""A wish is not a fact. Even by proving that a certain view is indispensable for living well, one proves merely that the view in

question is a salutary myth: one does not prove it to be true. Utility and truth are two entirely different things."
- Leo Strauss, German political philosopher

There is another, deeper problem, for conservative critics of nihilism. They tend to focus all of their energies on criticizing cultural nihilism; the public consensus that nothing matters. Perhaps cultural nihilism can be ameliorated by social change, though I think the problems relate more to material and economic concerns such as inequality, rather than academic and educational issues. But ameliorating cultural nihilism cannot eliminate it as a general philosophical prospect.

The great Oxford moral philosopher Derek Parfit has written an eloquent book *On What Matters* addressing this problem. Invoking Nietzsche amongst others, Parfit observes that nihilism is not simply a cultural problem. It is a very real meta-ethical and metaphysical issue that can only be resolved if we obtain an objective answer to the question of what "matters," or as Heidegger would put it, "why there is something instead of nothing at all." Peterson claims that we should draw on our biological and human history, seeing the values that have developed throughout history as a kind of evolutionary gift bequeathed to us by the past. Maybe. But that in itself does not provide an answer to whether these values are objective, or whether there is any real value in the world. It could be that at their root, these values simply emerged as a fortunate accident in an otherwise indifferent and valueless universe. In such a case, these values are just salutary myths that help us figure out who we are and what we should do. This is a good thing, but for us, not intrinsically.

This is a dour note to end on, but I will simply say this. Conservative critics like Peterson, Harper and others may wish to combat cultural nihilism. If that is their concern, I believe they should look more at economic and material systems they have hitherto left unscathed or even praised. But no political movement, self-help book, or transformation of the academy can resolve the philosophical problem of nihilism. For that we need a great deal more deep thinking into the problems of science and philosophy, and to my mind a more egalitarian distribution of wealth to enable a fuller flourishing of the human intellect for all.

The Problem with Identity Politics

Matt McManus

Just about everyone these days seems to have an opinion on identity politics, and it is almost universally negative. People on the right denigrate our shift to a politically correct culture in which certain ways of talking and thinking are denigrated as unacceptable and intolerant. They resent the so called social justice warriors who self-righteously condemn their political opponents as bigoted racists. On the left, there is a growing worry that nationalist alt-right movements are gaining momentum. People on the left worry that these alt-right movements thinly veil their xenophobia and racism behind the language of protectionism and security, and that they intend to take society in a regressive direction. All this is to say that no one seems happy about identity politics because almost everyone else seems to be engaging in it.

The United States naturally has a long history dealing with these issues, and takes no small pride in its status as an immigrant nation. But even here, there seems to be a growing sense that things have gone too far. One need only look at the immense anxieties raised over immigration and changing demographics over the last year for evidence. If even the United States isn't immune, who is?

To begin closing in on an answer, we need to start looking more deeply into the roots of identity politics. One of the things that gets lost in the heated debates is a close examination of the social trends that produce certain types of politics in the first place. Identity politics didn't emerge in a vacuum. There are a lot of reasons it has come to dominate political discourse, and a close look at them might indicate some of the ideological tensions on all sides of the political spectrum.

For instance, people on the alt-right often tend to segregate their commitment to unbridled capitalism from their social desire for less pandering to ethnic minorities. They see big government and liberal elites as responsible for creating a society that is at once too tolerant of foreign elements and too harsh towards the natives. What often isn't acknowledged is that markets play a huge role on both producing and deepening social fragmentation. This was recognized by great conservative thinkers like Max Weber and Joseph Schumpeter almost a century ago. Markets do not just passively react to what people want. The market is in the business of producing new values and novel ways of living, and making sure that people will buy into that. Over time, this transforms a society by creating ever more groups of people; bohemians, hipsters, cosmopolitan elites who want to jet around the world. In this way, markets help establish the conditions for the emergence of identity politics.

On the left, there is a different problem. Driven by historicist philosophies, people on the left have been quick to cast their ideological opponents as so bound up in systems of privilege that expressing their own needs and concerns can only be a front for a more nefarious agenda. The irony is that by calling out supposed racists and xenophobes everywhere, they helped produce the very tendencies they were concerned about. Rather than addressing the legitimate economic concerns of large groups of working class people who, whatever their ethnic identity, had a right to be heard, the left stood behind a Presidential candidate who castigated those who wouldn't vote for her as "deplorable." This illustrates how a myopic concern with ensuring greater equality for some can lead to the complete disdain and dismissal of others.

The irony is that people from all sides of the political spectrum are so quick to call out their opponents for deploying the rhetoric of identity politics, while often remaining blind to those features of their ideology that also perpetuate it. This suggests that there is no easy way to get out of identity politics these days, especially when we remain blind to the social trends that produce it, like markets and the growing popularity of historicist philosophies. It seems to me that the solution, after a long and bitter year, can only be to reflect more deeply on the tensions within our own convictions. Maybe that will help create a little empathy for the flaws we point out in our political rivals.

Why History Restarted: The Strange Warning of Francis Fukuyama and the Emergence of Postmodern Conservatism

Matthew McManus

Introduction

As we approach the 30th anniversary of the end of the Cold War, it is easy to get nostalgic for the comparative optimism and even triumphalism that pervaded Western societies. With the cessation of the struggle against the Soviet Union and its allies, a new era of neoliberal prosperity, respect for international human rights law, and general peace was to characterize the global order as humanity moved into the 21st century.

Few books captured the spirit of the time better than Francis Fukuyama's *The End of History and the Last Man.* Released in 1992 and based on his seminal 1989 essay released in *The National Interest,* Fukuyama argued that with the end of the Cold War and the collapse of Marxism as a viable alternative, liberal-democracy and free market capitalism had proven themselves the only viable model for political-economic organization. This implied that it would be increasingly embraced by states and peoples across the globe, who would be eager to be on the right side of the historical dialectic while also not having any real alternative model available to them.

Fukuyama was surprisingly non-dogmatic on this point. He acknowledged that some states and peoples might remain in rejecting a liberal democratic model of political organization and would strive to exist outside the globalizing power of the market. Some, like North Korea, might persist as outdated products of the previous epochal conflict between Marxism and liberal-democratic capitalism. Others might adopt theocratic regimes like the Ayatollahs of Iran or the Taliban in Afghanistan, eager to turn the clock back even further. But these outliers would be increasingly anomalous and unable to generate anything like the universal traction needed to challenge liberal-democracy and the market's ideological hegemony. This led him to the famous claim that history, as a struggle between different and viable models of political-economic organization, was at an end. Neo-liberal capitalism was now the only game in town.

The Intractability of the Fukuyama Thesis

Fukuyama's thesis was widely criticized at the time for its apparent triumphalism about the establishment of American dominance, its strange theoretical underpinning drawing on the German philosopher Hegel, and occasionally simply ignorance about the actual complexities orienting world affairs. Some of these critics, notably Samuel Huntington of "clash of civilizations" fame, attacked Fukuyama from the right. But by far the most vociferous critics came from the Left. Marxists like Perry Anderson argued that Fukuyama ignored the persistent and contradictory dynamics of capitalism, and the material impact this would have on future generations. The French philosopher of deconstruction, Jacques Derrida, famously agreed, claiming that it was sheer hubris to believe history was ending when so much violence, famine, and inequality, and exclusion persisted.

Some of these left wing criticisms had impressive heft to them. They observed where Fukuyama missed important practical or theoretical details, or criticized him for using sloppy generalizations where the reality was more complicated. And I think it is especially true to observe that the claim that history "ended" was more than a little abstract. For many starving individuals, and those in war torn countries such as Somalia and Yugoslavia, the idea that history was at an end must have seemed very quaint. It is also true that left wing alternatives to the neoliberal order never disappeared, though many took on a new post-Marxist form.

But many of the left-liberal criticisms were let down by a fundamental flaw: none of them were able to present a comprehensive and inspiring alternative to a liberal-democratic and capitalist model. Marxist philosopher Slavoj Zizek has long observed that, despite vociferous criticism, the lack of any comprehensive left wing alternative implied that most progressives secretly accepted the main thrust of Fukuyama's thesis. Whether they accepted it or not, most left liberal critics felt deep down that liberal capitalism was here to stay. Therefore many resigned themselves to one of two options. They either called for the liberal-democratic state and international institutions to soften the worst excesses of capitalism. This was the thrust of the broadly left-liberal and social democratic tradition of Habermas, Axel Honneth and others. Or critics on the liberal left turned to identity politics, hoping to develop a radical critique of the status quo that would mobilize what David Harvey calls various "militant particularisms" which would allow marginalized groups greater opportunity to participate in the liberal capitalist order. Unfortunately, without a systematic alternative, these critics on the "New Left" eventually caved to accepting the status quo; pushing for issues like more female CEOs, greater involvement by minorities in liberal politics etc. While many of these movements were vital in mitigating the worst effects of the status quo, and the struggles they embody must continue, they lacked the theoretical and popular support necessary to broadly challenge neo-liberal global hegemony.

These largely apologist movements have, unfortunately, come to dominate Western popular opinion on what the Left has to offer as an alternative to the neo-liberal world order. This is in spite of the fact that many significant movements developed which to this day offer us clues on what a post-neoliberal order might look like. In Mexico (my current home address) the Zapatista movement, established in 1994 in the state of Chiapas, reacted against the neo-liberal reforms of the 1990s by establishing "bottom up" communes dedicated to participatory government and protecting the rights of aboriginals and women. More recently, Greece's Syriza party took an initially strong stand against the implementation of structural reform which undermined the welfare state to ensure the payment of debts to the international banking system. And an impressive host of left wing philosophers, from Roberto Unger to David Harvey, have developed novel and inspiring systematic alternatives to neoliberalism which can provide us with theoretical guidance in the future. But so far none of these movements and intellectual trends have garnered enough popular support and influence to seriously challenge the global hegemony of neoliberal governance.

So, despite criticism, for a long time Fukuyama's thesis has remained alive and well. The Left was simply unable to develop a comprehensive and inspiring alternative that could do more than ameliorate the worst impacts of neoliberal governance. These were important struggles, but could not change the status quo. To begin thinking of how we might do that, it is worth looking at another dimension of Fukuyama's thought which has been rarely addressed and should give us pause. This was his argument that, if history was going to start again, the energy to restart it would come from the right rather than the left. The right would restart history by mobilizing identity to counteract the boredom and lack of meaning which characterized post-historical societies. I think this is precisely what we are seeing today, and demonstrates the need (and potential) of the left to seize the energies now corralled by the right and move them in a more progressive direction.

The Last Man

"'What is love? What is creation? What is longing? What is a star?'" -- so asks the Last Man, and blinks. The earth has become small, and on it hops the Last Man, who makes everything small. His species is ineradicable as the flea; the Last Man lives longest." Nietzsche, *Thus Spoke Zarathustra*

Fukuyama was never the triumphalist stooge that he has so often been caricatured as. Many on the left, despite hostility towards his claims, have been unable to move past his arguments in any substantial way beyond modest calls for reform or lapsing into post-modern skepticism and identity politics. Interestingly enough, it is Fukuyama himself who provided one of the keys to understanding why his central thesis about the end of history would not hold forever. As early as his first essay on the topic Fukuyama observed:

"...I can feel in myself, and see in others around me, a powerful nostalgia for the time when history existed. Such nostalgia, in fact, will continue to fuel competition and conflict even in the post-historical world for some time to come. Even though I recognize its inevitability, I have the most ambivalent feelings for the civilization that has been created in Europe since 1945, with its North Atlantic and Asian offshoots. Perhaps this very prospect of centuries of boredom at the end of history will serve to get history started once again."

Later in his major book *The End of History and the Last Man*, Fukuyama drew on Nietzsche's writings about the "last man" to deepen these arguments. The last man was a person with no higher orientation in life than his private satisfaction. He was disinterested in the broader culture or any grand projects, largely irreligious, and not especially curious. The fundamental characteristic of the last man was his concern, first and foremost, with "health." This was Nietzsche's metaphor for not being concerned with higher goals other than bodily pleasures, especially great struggles over meaning and identity. The last man would be the inhabitant of a post-ideological world; largely comfortable on the outside, but nihilistic at its very core. Fukuyama argued that many on the right, after recognizing this lack of meaning in their lives, might strive to bring history back again in order to alleviate this sense of meaninglessness and apathy. Of course, this would entail the return of war, ideological conflict, and social division.

The Emergence and Rise of Postmodern Conservatism

Today, with the emergence of what I call postmodern conservatism, we are witnessing exactly this trend. Postmodern conservatives largely come from the most privileged groups in history, usually belonging to an identity that has historically been dominant in society. But, facing pressure from neoliberal forces of globalization, and the affiliated labor mobility, immigration, and demands for multicultural toleration consonant with liberal rights doctrines, these postmodern conservatives increasingly feel that their dominant place in society is under threat. They see no way to rectify this within the parameters of neoliberal capitalism, and resent its "elite" intellectual defenders who mask their arguments about its merits under the pretense of so called "objectivity" and "reason." So postmodern conservatives increasingly reject the very notions of objectivity and reason, since they are so affiliated with "elite" liberal groups indifferent to their concerns. Instead, they appeal to the knowledge and values of their given "identity." This includes claiming that immigrants are destroying the country and committing great acts of violence, that nation states once dominated by their identity are increasingly becoming "Islamified" by oncoming waves of Muslims, that foreigners in Brussels and around the world are pulling the strings of national policy, and so on. Whether this is true or not from some "objective" standpoint is a matter of indifference to postmodern conservatives. They *feel* that it is true, and those who align with their identity do so as well.

Postmodern conservatives have increasingly found political spokesmen to articulate their positions. Donald Trump, Nigel Farage, Marine Le Pen, Victor Orban of Hungary, and the Freedom and Justice Party of Poland, have all mobilized apocalyptic rhetoric about the collapse of traditional values as the traditional identities affiliated with a given nation have disappeared. Postmodern conservative politicians deploy the rhetoric of victimization and resentment for the retrenchment of power and authority in the hands of heartland citizens-a shorthand for the person who shares *our* identity because they look, speak, and think like we do. The fact that the identities under attack are far more privileged than the immigrants blamed, and that far from being driven by the people, postmodern conservative movements have often been widely authoritarian and anti-democratic in practice, is a point that is largely ignored. Because postmodern conservatives already distrust "elite" intellectual opinion, it has been very easy for their political spokesmen to ridicule counter arguments as "fake news," "alternative facts," and their proponents as not being in touch with the "heartland." This is an extremely dangerous development in political culture. All politicians lie at some point; that is not news. What makes postmodern conservatism so dangerous is its indifference to the very idea of truth.

Conclusion

The emergence of postmodern conservatism as a new force in history proper indicates the need to take Fukuyama's arguments about the "Last Man" more seriously. We are facing a dangerous moment where right wing populism, from the United States to Italy, is a very real threat to both justice and truth. But it also presents us with new opportunities to challenge that status quo. The anger and resentment channeled by postmodern conservatives stems from a place of legitimate grievances against the harshness and inequities of neoliberal hegemony. These can be channeled in more progressive directions.

We are increasingly faced with a world where inequality grows ever more rampant and where even the minimal safety net offered by the welfare state is breaking down. The political energies unleashed by that can be harnessed by effective left wing movements who can present real and inspiring alternatives to the status quo. My suspicion would be that we should look more closely at the examples offered by the Zapatista movements, successful left democratic parties like Syriza, and the theoretical work of thinkers like Unger and Harvey for inspiration. These can help us develop ideas, strategies, and proposals which will do a better job of convincing others that structural change is possible. To my mind, this is the most pressing task we on the Left face as we move deeper into the uncertainties of the 21st century.

On American Violence and Alienation

Matthew McManus

Introduction

In an article for the *National Review*, noted conservative Ben Shapiro argued that the victims in the recent Parkland School shooting were too immature to think through these issues rationally. Admittedly they did gain some first-hand experience with the consequences of gun culture when a former student tried to take their lives from them, but this didn't magically give them unique insights into how government policy around guns should be oriented. Moreover, Shapiro accused the left of having an "emotional" reaction to this issue, and exploiting the young victims of the shooting to engender a similarly emotional reaction from the public. This seems to be Shapiro's iteration of the now standard Republican accusations that their opponents attempt to politicize the gun issue whenever there is a mass shooting; since clearly the honest thing to do is to send hopes and prayers before cashing the next NRA donation.

Republican Arguments about School Shootings

Shapiro's typically trite observations bring to mind a statement made by philosopher and psychoanalyst Erich Fromm many decades ago: that in a truly sick society, madness can assume the guise of rationality. Shapiro speaks for many Republicans when he implies that his position on firearms is the only rational one, contrasted with the "emotional" reactions of weak-willed victims and mourners. The irony is that for many the "right to bear arms" is justified by little more than bias towards the status quo. Supporters make the tautologous claim that they should have a right to bear arms because the Constitution *says* they have the right to bear arms. This position is held with such pious fundamentalism that leading Republicans such as the President are debating whether the most practical solution to school shootings is arming teachers. This is a magnificently strange position in which the apparent solution to gun violence in schools is apparently more guns in schools. The banality and danger of such a solution boggles the imagination.

Of course, Republicans have not limited themselves to simply proposing more bad policies. Some have taken it upon themselves to explain why school shootings have occurred and to concurrently justify gun culture. Dana Loesch, spokeswoman for the NRA, is a notable recent example. She invoked the favored line in this case: that gun violence is caused by individuals with mental illnesses. Other Republicans have had more esoteric arguments. Donald Trump resurrected the long discredited claim that violent video games are to blame. Matt Bevin, the Governor of Kentucky, blamed music and pornographic images for destroying the "fabric of America." In each of these cases, the causes of gun violence are localized to culture or individual determinants in order to shield the weapons industry from any blame. And of course, the favorite targets of socially conservative Republicans-from modern music to popular Millennial forms of entertainment-are castigated as the true culprits for their role in destroying the fabric of society.

The irony is that there is a degree of truth to these claims. Republicans are wrong to claim that the mass production and dissemination of deadly weapons across society is not to blame for gun violence. One need only look at the far lower rates of gun violence in any number of developed states with stricter gun laws for evidence. The tendency to believe that analogous laws would not work in the United States is an extremely bizarre formulation of American exceptionalism. However, Republicans are right that the broader culture is in part to blame for what has happened. To understand the roots of gun violence, social actors need to look more deeply at its roots in the larger culture and history of American society. But Republicans are right for all the wrong reasons.

American Violence

The modern Republican Party is defined in no small part by its myopic partisanship. This is why so many of its chosen culprits for gun violence-madness, video games, pornography, modern music-seem to have been copied wholesale from a segment of Bill O'Reilly's now defunct television show. No attempt is made at a more general and structural examination into the roots of American violence; probably because doing so would itself undermine so many cherished Republican idolatries.

Earlier, I invoked Erich Fromm's comment that in a sick society, madness would resemble a form of rationality. This observation referenced the Fascist states of Italy and Nazi Germany, where as Walter Benjamin put it in "The Work of Art in the Age of Mechanical Reproduction," society had turned itself into a kind of mass circus. Violence, prejudice, and hyper-partisan nationalism were all encouraged and transformed into propaganda and spectacle. This dangerous society emerged in a capitalist context where people were increasingly alienated from one another. Capitalism, as a revolutionary form of production and distribution, had destroyed earlier and more communal forms of life, many of them organized around religion. It had replaced them with a society in which each individual found themselves in competition with all others in a war for survival and standing within a hierarchy. For Benjamin and Fromm, it was no surprise that in such a hyper alienated context individuals would feel a deep loneliness and resentment. They would find it appealing to turn to violent but entertaining forms of political association that would provide them with a sense of meaning and community, while also offering the opportunity for publicity and fame by clamping down on others. In such a society, individuals would direct their psychic energy towards a paradoxical activity: feeling powerful by publically degrading the lives of others. This, of course, reached its apex with the Genocide.

America today looks ever more like the type of societies described by Fromm and Benjamin. Many alienated individuals turn to gun violence as a way to feel powerful and warrant attention. It is not often acknowledged that many of these individuals come from broken and poor homes and have few prospects in life. Understanding the roots of this violence means looking more deeply into the culture than just blaming video games and music. It will mean examining how the economic and political order we inhabit produces individuals who feel they have no other option but to go down in a blaze of hatred.

The Culture War is Not Taking Place: On the Technological Contingency of Postmodern Conservatism

Dylan De Jong and Matt McManus

Introduction

We are now approaching the 30th anniversary of the end of the Cold War and proclamations that the "end of history" was nigh. Looking back, the triumphalist sentiments of the liberal 1990s seem positively misguided. Battles about what social values should be accepted, what books should be read on campus, and even the language that can be used in polite society seem to rage onwards as part of the so called "culture wars." Indeed, the culture war seems to be reaching a fever pitch across the Western world. In Hungary, Victor Orban is seeking reelection to retrench his anti-refugee "illiberal democracy." In the United Kingdom, the debate about Brexit and how best to protect British sovereignty carries on. In Poland, the Law and Justice Party continues to pursue its campaign to re-Christianize the country and purge it of foreign influences. And of course, in the United States the farcical display of Trumpism continues to play itself out.

Obviously, these trends are worrying and have a real significance. Our point isn't to dismiss that. Instead, we want to look at the digital roots of the culture war and demonstrate how its most aggressive militants are motivated more by the hyperreal influx of ideological products than by a cool look at reality. Despite the tremendous lack of evidence that Western civilization is in any way under threat, what we term post-modern conservatism has emerged in digital mediums to combat this decline under the auspices of "culture war." Post-modern conservatism is characterized by all the hyperbole and disconnection from reality that one would expect from a movement that emerged on the internet. But this does not mean that it is unable to impact the real world. One of the concerning features of postmodern conservatism has been its push to transform reality in line with the unreal by mobilizing traditional identity to attack the specter of the "other."

The Culture War Isn't Taking Place: Digital Echo Chambers

The battlefields of the culture war are digital, primarily social media feeds, podcasts, and the various comments sections. The basic vocabulary of the conflict has, in a relatively short time, become concrete"radical left," "alt-right," "social justice warrior," "mainstream or liberal media"--such that the use of any of these terms immediately identifies them with a tribe, without the need of any additional context; the rain barrels of left and right catch all.

Yet the culture war is not really taking place; rather, it appears to be taking place precisely because it isn't. Social media feeds (particularly those of YouTube, Facebook, and Twitter) produce polarized antagonism by design. The content that is most likely to be rewarded and thrust into visibility is that which provokes immediate reaction; that is, norm-deviance increases the likelihood of propagation. News consists of the extraordinary, the exceptional, the excessive, and the scandalous--that which is unexpected is that which is most likely to incite a reaction.

Norm-deviant communication circuits are produced and enabled by personalized feeds, wherein interacting with some content (by viewing, liking, commenting etc.) is rewarded with more associated content. Over time, reinforcing a user's personal ranking algorithm causes the genetic drift of the vocabulary, opinions, and associations of one's nodular tribe, such that their communication becomes increasingly detached from the aggregate status quo, and increasingly antagonistic to nodular tribes with contrary vocabulary, opinions and associations. These circuits are commonly known as "filter bubbles" or "echo chambers," which are isolated communication circuits wherein nodes of users' feeds normalize the extraordinary, exceptional, excessive and scandalous. All that becomes visible is the most deviant and polarizing content: a simulation of war.

The Polarization of Discourse and The Emergence of Post-Modern Conservatism

We should clarify, even as our hyperreal culture war is being waged among the ranking algorithms of social media feeds, it is not the sufficient cause for polarized discourse itself, for as J.S. Mill observed 150 years ago, "in the human mind, one-sidedness has always been the rule, and many-sidedness the exception." However, a user can find him or herself in a hyperreal feedback loop quite easily. If you require convincing, click your way to YouTube in a private browsing window, type in your boogeyman of choice--e.g. alt-right, social justice warrior, or liberal media--and let the autoplay carry you to the battlefields of hyperreal antagonism, where the heroes of one's tribe OWN or DESTORY the other's. For many, it seems, these exchanges come to represent truly personal and pressing concerns for their culture's future.

Given the technological contingency of the situation, we wish to focus on the emergence of what we have termed post-modern conservatism. Fundamentally, this association is one of nostalgia and antagonistic identity politics, and its heroes are prolific social media celebrities who have strategically or unwittingly used the basic operations of feed algorithms to become authorities in the eyes of their followers. Truth and falsity in postmodern conservatism is largely a matter of a tribal vocabulary in opposition to what is usually reduced to "the radical left."

To illustrate: campus protests demanding safe-spaces are rare, just as white supremacist rallies are rare. Yet when such events are offered up as content to a feed which privileges norm-deviant content, they are virtually guaranteed to be made visible. The occurrences of these events need not be subject to corroboration with the status quo of offline reality, where they are unlikely to occur, because the reality of social media is generated as a closed system of digital information. Relative to "news," offline reality is drab and predictable. Enabled by the feed, however, the most extreme positions become normalized, supplanting the relative banality of the majority with the figures of "radical postmodern Marxists" or "white nationalist authoritarians." Although no such extremes exist, they are far overrepresented in the rhetoric of their antagonists due to the visibility rewarded by the feed. These trends are exaggerated, and seen as indicatory that the cultural fabric of society is being fundamentally changed. Often this is associated with implicit fears about social fragmentation: the core values of societies are being abandoned as society increasingly liberalizes in line with the progressive doctrines advocated by out of touch "elites" such as intellectuals and through the demands of unnatural minority groups such as members of the LGBTQ community. More insidiously, postmodern conservatives will point to the ever growing number of foreigners, who bring with them alien values and ways of living, as another source of social fragmentation. These exaggerated fears, stoked within hyperreal mediums, are then used to mobilize the ethnic identity of those who hold to "traditional values."

Conclusion: Postmodern Conservatism's Identity Politics

Though it emerged in the echo chambers of the internet, postmodern conservatism has since achieved considerable popular and political success. This is a very worrying trend. Post-modern conservatism is characterized by the hyperbolic and apocalyptic sense that the core values of society are collapsing and social fragmentation deepening. The blame for this is cast on unpopular "elite" groups like intellectual and marginalized communities such as LGBTQ groups and ethnic minorities drawn to developed countries. To fight against them, post-modern conservatism mobilizes traditionally powerful identities in society, stoking the resentment at being victimized by those who do not hold to their values. Their calls for a retrenchment of tradition are cast along the lines of identity, rather than through appeals to truth or objectivity, because identity and its affiliated values cannot be challenged by the traditional means available in "normal" political discourse. What this means, of course, is that postmodern conservatives have developed their own form of identity politics. But unlike the more pluralistic identity politics often affiliated with left-wing postmodernism, postmodern conservatism adopts a homogenizing stance towards society. Postmodern conservatives want power to remain with those who have traditionally enjoyed it so they can roll back perceived social fragmentation and restore the core values of society. It is in the interest of all of us to make sure they don't get it.

Trumpism and Loneliness: The Rise of Vulgar Authoritarianism

Matt McManus

Loneliness

In Hannah Arendt's pioneering book *The Origins of Totalitarianism*, she criticized the failure of many to understand the appeals of fascism to modern citizens. She wrote that many observers gave fairly rote justifications for its rise and appeal in an apparently advanced and enlightened country like Germany, the birthplace of Goethe, Kant, and Beethoven. Some claimed that it was the depressed economy which was responsible. Others in the German context pointed to defeat and humiliation in the First World War. Some reactionary conservatives claimed that it was declining moral standards and the collapse of religiosity. And Arendt accepted that many of these might have something to do with it. But her ultimate explanation was far simpler and yet strangely more acute. Modern Germans were just lonely.

The technologically oriented modern world, focused on the production of wealth and new economic values, had driven many Germans from their homes in rural areas. There they had expected to grow into secure jobs in traditional forms of work whose ancestry went back centuries. Instead, they found themselves in big cities where they knew no one and were exposed to forms of life with which they had no familiarity, and which seemed to evolve and metastasize from day to day. Coupled with the realization that the myth of endless capitalist expansion was simply that, a mythology brutally desacralized with the advent of Depression and unemployment, countless Germans found themselves alone and poor in a world that seemed strange and unreal to them. In this context, their capacity for resentment and radicalization deepened and could gnaw at itself in bitter isolation. It was only a matter of time before many of these same Germans gravitated to the simplifying but rhetorically powerful movements which promised them belonging, prosperity, and of course, revenge against the manipulative alien parties who had infected their country.

Today, Arendt's analysis still has a great deal to teach us about the appeal of hard right movements to lonely individuals. Much has been written about the rise of Trumpism: its relativism, its appeal to traditional values to efface all standard political conventions, its vulgarity, its populism, but relatively little attention has been paid to its psycho-social foundations beyond traditional appeals to working class ennui and economic malaise. Here Arendt can still be our teacher. But we must update her insights considerably by looking at how our now post-modern technological world engenders new but still seductive hard right movements.

Technology and Capitalism

It seems strange today to think of how anyone could be lonely. Technology, especially telecommunications and the internet, have brought about a global village where billions of people can interconnect with one another in an instant. Often all that is required is a cell phone with a decent enough data plan. People are connecting with one another at a rate that would bewilder even such prophets of the post-modern world as Marshall McLuhan and Jean Baudrillard. Moreover, the economy is booming. After a recessionary dip in the last 2000s, the 2010s have seen recovery and job expansion in the United States and many other OECD countries.

Any yet hard right movements like Trumpism thrive because people say they are deeply anxious and losing their country. They feel alienated and like they no longer connect with their communities. Many claim that Western Civilization itself-whatever that means-is under assault by hordes of turbaned and hooded immigrants bringing foreign religions and customs. How is this possible? With immense capacities to communicate, and interconnected economy, and Western Civilization still mostly retaining its position as globally hegemonic, how is it that these hard right movements exist? I believe that the answer lies in the political and economic processes of post-modern capitalism and its alliance with the powers of technology. Just as in Arendt's day, these same forces continue to propel a culture of loneliness and anxiety. But they do so in a unique way.

In the United States and other Western countries, reactionary conservatives have long made idols of both Christendom and the dollar. They wanted a white, Christian society organized according to traditional mores that were widely approved by democratic majorities. At the same time they wanted robust capitalist societies in which barriers to capital expansion and wealth creation were liquidated as rapidly as possible. What was never accepted was the fundamental tension between these two positions. The stability of a traditional way of life is in no small part dependent on maintaining forms of wealth creation and their affiliated technologies to the extent possible. But one of the features of capitalization, especially in the post-modern era where technology enables the movement of wealth and the creation of new industries with unparalleled rapidity, has been precisely to upend these traditional forms of wealth creation and their affiliated technologies. At points capitalist firms will move themselves around the globe. At others they will simply outdate industries; coal being an ideal example. These will demolish traditional forms of wealth creation and the communities which depend on them. And this is just the tendencies on the surface.

Echoing observations by Edmund Burke decades before, in the middle of the 19th century Karl Marx wrote that in capitalism "everything that is solid melts into air." He was referring to the tendency of capitalism to upend traditional forms of life and their affiliated mores. Strangely, it has largely been the most conservative critics who acknowledged this tendency and sought to explain it. Writers such as Max Weber, Joseph Schumpeter, and George Grant recognized that capitalism-for all its variations-has an uncanny ability to transform societies by liquidating barriers, including moral barriers, to the pursuit of profit. In some circumstances this could mean liberalizing the public sphere. In other circumstances, it meant colonizing the globe to establish new markets and tear down competition.

We can see the impacts of this every day. We live in a society where capitalist firms continuously create new values through the production of new products and technologies which are affiliated with diverse ways of life. In effect, capitalism produces social difference by encouraging people to express their individuality through consumption. Bohemian hipsters assume their identity through purchasing the right clothes, drinking the right beer, and pushing for the legalized sale of narcotics. Emancipated women are expected to earn a big salary, wear the right clothes, and buy cars that would make a yuppie blush. And of course, we have a President who has transformed the very idea of truth into a kind of marketable value, determined by popularity and campaign donations. And this is simply the case in the Western world. It boggles the imagination to conceive of the social transformations wrought by capital in economic giants such as China and India, where growing disparities in wealth and development have led to immensely different ways of living in various parts of the country.

Trumpism and Capitalism

We can now bring this analysis full circle to update Arendt's analysis of loneliness and the appeal of fascism. Modern capitalism continuously revolutionizes both the forms of wealth creation and the affiliated technologies present in a society, and the values that society professes. Far from being an ally of traditional, "Christian" society, it has demolished even the possibility of tradition. And it will continue to do so at an accelerating rate.

Recognizing this and dealing with it extensively would require a deep rooted commitment to critique and analysis of contemporary trends in political economy and our growing dependence on technology. But this is rarely undertaken, in no small part because the powers that be benefit from these very tendencies and have no interest in seeing them abetted. The consequence is that the many individuals who are increasingly outdated by these trends, and left alone in a society they no longer recognize, turn to the modern technologies which helped render them obsolete. There, they do not turn to the global polis and the wealth of information provided by modern technologies. Instead these individuals look inward, towards groups and individuals who feel the same sense of alienation and loneliness. Rather than look to the complexity of these social trends, and recognizing the breadth of the problem, these individuals find powerful figures like Trump and Steve Bannon who are willing to profit from, and direct, the powers caged in their resentment. The finger is pointed not at the roots of social trends, but at its symptoms and critics. Migrants, leftists, intellectuals and employees in the knowledge sector, cosmopolitans and so on. These provide an easy and vulnerable outlet for lashing out. So a few hundred Muslims wearing a burka, or a Professor teaching a class on post-colonial theory for 2 hours a week, become the subject of paranoiac projects. They are tormentors who emerge to tear down society. All the while, what is ignored is that figures like Trump and Bannon, who deploy the might of capital and technology to advance their own power and egos, are the most individualized catalysts for the real forces undermining tradition and society. The vulgar authoritarianism of Trumpism is the result of these radical trends in our society. It gives expression to the resentment of the lonely and alienated whom these trends have left behind, and deliberately channels their energy against the weak and vulnerable to prevent recognition of the real roots of the problem.

Conservatism in the Age of Twitter

Matt McManus

Examining the overall state of conservatism today is one of the major purposes of this book. Doing so will give us a better sense of how we moved from the boring but stately conservative parties of the 1990s to the post-modern pastiche of scandal and outrage that is Trump-Brexit-Orban conservatism. I think there are three types of conservatives in the Anglosphere today. The first are the traditionalists. Then there are the radicals. And finally there are what I have been calling the post-modern conservatives, who are currently the ascendant group.

Traditionalist conservatives include writers like Bill Kristol in the United States, Jordan Peterson in Canada, and Roger Scruton in the United Kingdom. Each of them supports conservative positions from a different philosophical perspective, but has reached similar conclusions about the state of conservatism today. Their outlook was nicely summarized in a recent op-ed Scruton produced for *The New York Times* on Donald Trump and tariffs. In his article, Scruton evokes nostalgia for the refined conservatism of Thomas Jefferson and Margaret Thatcher, complains that Trumpism is vulgarizing politics with its lack of intellectual substance, and then observes that American conservatives no longer seem to care much about market capitalism and free trade. He concludes by arguing that at best Trump has a "distorted" vision of conservatism. The implication is that Scruton wants everyone to get back on the right track. I think Scruton, and those like him, are correct that Donald Trump's conservatism is "distorted" and breaks with the past. It is therefore not surprising that many conservatives like him revolt against these shifts. But I think these traditionalist conservatives don't spend enough time really analyzing why figures like Trump and other right wing populists have emerged across the Western world. There is a reactionary quality to their critiques of right wing populism, as if it were nothing but a few vulgar demagogues who successfully conned their populations into buying into fundamentally non-conservative ideas. To understand why conservatism has changed we are going to need a deeper analysis.

This is where the radical conservatives come in; figures like Alasdair Macintyre (not quite a conservative but a big intellectual influence), and writers for *The American Conservative*. Perhaps the most articulate of these radical conservatives is Patrick Deneen, whose great book *Why Liberalism Failed* has provoked furious commentary on all sides of the political spectrum. Deneen argues that for too long commentators on both the progressive left and what I have called the traditionalist conservative right have ignored fundamental tensions within their more basic doctrine: liberalism itself. Progressives accepted liberal morals and markets, but wanted to temper the latter with a few welfare programs to help the poor and needy. Traditionalist conservatives also accepted liberal morals and markets, but wanted to temper the former by conserving a few culturally specific traditions and hierarchies. Politics in developed nations tended to consist of tediously passing the baton between these two groups and their respective political parties.

What Deneen argues is that liberalism is beset by more basic tensions than either progressive leftists or traditionalist conservatives recognized. Their faith in liberal markets meant that both groups presumed that the middle and lower classes would accept immense and often unfair levels of economic inequality so long as their standard of living continued to increase. Much of this faith stemmed from endless faith in technological advancement and how its benefits would trickle down. What liberals on all ends of the political spectrum didn't recognize is that technological and economic transformations are fundamentally changing the way we communicate and interact with one another. Technology and markets have radically globalized the world, tearing up old cultures, traditions and values as they advance. Economist Joseph Schumpeter called this process "creative destruction." Resentment about social and economic inequality, and the limited political power that comes from being at the bottom of the pecking order, can now spread and fester across the internet. Communication bubbles form where the resentful and disaffected are continuously exposed to click bait sensationalism and hyper-partisan rhetoric. According to Deneen, all this has occurred not because liberalism has failed, but because it has succeeded. And it is what traditionalist conservatives who still want a return to the status quo of faith in markets, trickle-down economics, and maintaining a few cultural practices have failed to see.

This brings me to the third and now ascendant type of conservatism in the developed world: post-modern conservatism. Post-modern conservatism emerges in the Age of Twitter. Resentful individuals who feel disconnected from the politics of their countries, and who are paranoid about the rapid changes transforming their societies, come together using the same technologies that helped bring about those changes. In digital media and partisan networks like Breitbart and Fox News they find hyper-partisan figures willing to ignore facts, stoke an angry identity politics, and direct their followers against readily available enemies responsible for their lot: immigrants, academics, the media, and status quo politicians. These post-modern conservatives are the product of the socio-economic and technological changes that have transformed our world. Their solutions can't do anything to get at the root of these changes since post-modern conservatives rely on them to achieve success (what would Trump be without a hyper-partisan internet?). What makes these post-modern conservatives dangerous is what they will do in lieu of actually fixing these problems.

Post-Modern Politics and Post-Modern Conservatism

Dylan DeJong and Erik Tate

Introduction

Many conservatives seem unperturbed that in their spirited defense against the alleged evils of identity politics and cultural relativism, many on the right in the United States and abroad—from Marine Le-Pen's National Front to Viktor Orban's "illiberal democracy" in Hungary to the surge of the anti-muslim/ immigrant *Lega Nord* in Italy's 2018 election—have embraced an exclusionary identity politics whose primary concern is the restoration of their in-group's privilege. In place of an appeal to common values, compromise for public welfare, and rational civil discourse, we find nationalist xenophobia, conspiracy peddling, and reactionary invective against any who criticize these zero-sum attitudes. With this uncompromising appeal to narrative over argument and to group identity, we are witnessing the emergence of a postmodern conservatism.

Postmodernism is not first and foremost an intellectual movement (although its inner dynamics were first consciously or unconsciously understood and expressed by intellectuals and artists). Postmodernism is a historically situated hermeneutic perspective which maintains that objective or universalist considerations, particularly meta-ethical standards for making moral judgments, are not all they are cracked up to be, and thus should be cracked up, or at least subject to critique. With the effacement of those standards that Nietzsche called the "tables of values," many turn to subjective identity as a source of stability and normative authority in what feels like an increasingly unmoored reality.

Identity and Postmodern Conservatism

The growing cultural emphasis on identity may appear to contrast the expectations of many postmodern theorists, who sought first and foremost to problematize the very idea of identity itself. But identity, like the nation state in relation to globalization, has proven rather more intractable than many anticipated. Anxiety is a byproduct of social and economic mobility, as the dissolution of established strictures makes one responsible for their destiny. The first great philosopher of postmodernism, Friedrich Nietzsche, called for the individual, creative revaluation of all values, and he was aware of the responsibility this would entail. In response, those too weak to shoulder the burden would succumb to a form of nihilism, rather than realize its emancipatory possibilities. These individuals would become vapid and passive "last men"; content to idly pass time consuming, rather than creating. These individuals would be largely indifferent to the world, isolated, concerned with "health" and their private satisfactions. They would will no great projects, and exist as willing nihilists passively absorbing entertainment and spectacle, and contentedly belonging to groups without risk.

Today, we are witness to the reaction against a culture of "last men" by post-modern conservatives. The notion of identity is being rejuvenated by postmodernists on the right and left who see it as a political category by which they can stave off the nihilism of neoliberal culture. As we shall argue, reactionary authoritarianism aims to halt the erosion of the nation-state by advocating an exclusionary form of identity politics. Postmodern conservatives embody this impetuousness, regarding neo-liberal society as decadent and wracked with interests inimical to their own. In keeping with the characteristics of postmodernism, they are indifferent to "objective" epistemic or meta-ethical standards for assessing behavior, and instead revert to reactionary narratives railing against corrupt elites and ill-intentioned immigrants who, together, are conspiring to take over the world that once belonged to *us*. Thus, according to this narrative, liberal elites promulgate fake news which needs to be countered by "alternative facts" that fit the presuppositions of post-modern conservatives. Rather than develop a novel table of values, which includes epistemic, aesthetic, and meta-ethical standards, to supplant that of the "liberal elite" (which include professional politicians, the academic class, and the press) and buttress their "alternative facts," postmodern conservatives appeal to traditional narratives of identity and values as a rallying point for resistance against those who threaten the interests of their tribe. They are able to do so very effectively because of the rise of new media.

Tribal Signaling and Social Media

In the Trump-Era conservative media intentionally seeks to overwhelm the critical sensibilities of the citizenry to make them doubt the existence of a knowable truth. The conservative media is a "giant fog machine designed to confuse and disorient people," according to conservative political commentator Charlie Sykes. The postmodern conservative narrative does not seek to differentiate fact from fiction; rather, it distinguishes us from them. This narrative differentiation of in-group from out-group generates patterns of behavior and communication—signals—such that one's fellow ideologues can be immediately recognized. Tribal signaling predates even tribes, and figures of every political stripe adopt them. Some are explicit (the salute, the armband, the baseball cap) and some less so (the accent, the name-drop, the euphemism). Now of course the signaling itself is nothing new; however, there is one novel technology/tool that has transformed this practice, one for which postmodern conservatives have developed an undeniable proclivity: social media.

Social media, in most every structural sense, appears to be

like the realization of a cyberpunk's Utopia: free communication available indiscriminately across class, national, and now even linguistic boundaries. In 1996, John Perry Barlow declared that "We are creating a world that all may enter without privilege or prejudice accorded by race, economic power, military force, or station of birth," but now, social media has very much enabled the hyperpolarization of politics, lack of critical engagement and the emergence of nigh-impenetrable echo chambers. Within these communication circuits, postmodern conservatism has found a safe space for its narrative.

Norm-deviant communication circuits emerge from and are enabled by the feeds of YouTube, Facebook, and Twitter. Interacting with some content (by viewing, liking, commenting etc.) is rewarded with associated content. Over time, this reinforces a user's preferences in the form of a personalized ranking algorithm which causes the congealment of a tribe's signaling vocabulary. Postmodern conservative signals are strangely consistent even across continents. Their terms include: liberals, borders and immigrants, the liberal agenda, the fake or mainstream media, globalists, patriots, elites, the deep state, feminism and an obsession with "opposing" politicians and celebrities and their nefarious activities (proven, unproven, fabricated—it makes no difference). George Soros, Hillary Clinton, and EU leaders seem particularly vilified from Hungary to the United States.

Refreshing the feed carries us deep into the battlefields of hyperreal antagonism, where the heroes of one's tribe OWN or DESTORY those of the others.' For many, these exchanges come to represent an existential defense of their culture's future, and nationalist undertones are always present. In a narrative that can only be described as paranoid, postmodern conservatives exploit a haunting anxiety of invasion or domination. They name and signify enemies, projecting/attaching that anxiety over an absent or ambiguous otherness onto/to coherent groups—

the elite caste, the mainstream media, radicals, and, perhaps most unfortunately, immigrants, all of which form a unified conspiracy to liquidate "us."

One's allegiance to the tribe is further determined by a function present in all feed-based social media: the like button. As contributes to the ranking of content, user decisions must be binary (social media within which a user may react positively or not at all) or ternary (social media within which a user may react positively, negatively, or not at all). There is therefore a very simple script if one is to be a good tribe member: like/favorite/upvote what the tribe favors, dislike/downvote/ignore what the tribe does not favor, and you can only act as you will regarding issues where the tribe has no stance. A metric of veracity or truth never enters the process. All that is required is to respond to tribal signaling in accordance with the tribe's table of values.

Conclusion: Paranoia and Politics

This tribalism peaks with the postmodern conservative rallying cry about the need to defend Western civilization itself. This is exemplified in a speech by Donald Trump—the postmodern conservative in chief—given in Warsaw in July 2017. Trump warned of the myriad internal dangers facing "Western Civilization" including those who "sap its confidence" and called for a return to "culture, faith, and tradition." For others, the identity appealed to corresponds to race and ethnicity, and the need to establish racial ethno-states for protection against the corruption of the other. During the Charlottesville protests, for example, hundreds of white nationalists railed against the Jews, Muslims, and blacks who sought to "replace" them. A similar logic underpins Viktor Orban's January 2018 comments about Muslim "invaders" who seek to create "parallel societies" alongside the traditionally dominant in-group, arguing that they cannot co-exist.

The paranoia befalling many developed countries means

that postmodern conservatives are enjoying an effective surge across the globe. With the simple promise of defending the status quo which benefits a dominant in-group, they have gained political power at the expense of marginalized peoples and movements, and continue attempts to seize state power across North America and Europe. The desire for state power among postmodern conservatives is derived from two aims: Firstly, despite its erosion under the pressures of globalization, the state and its institutional apparatus remains the most readily available tool for a given localized identity to manifest its power and reestablish its domestic sovereignty. Giorgio Agamben noted this in his seminal work, *Homo Sacer*, on the state of exception, and the means by which sovereignty is determined by the capacity to exclude individuals. Secondly, controlling the state apparatuses has an ideological significance because its boundaries are often regarded as co-extensive with the legitimate geographic entitlements of the identities postmodern conservatives deem to be under threat. Once they seize control, postmodern conservatives deepen the effects of postmodern culture and efface any epistemic, aesthetic, and meta-ethical standards by which their opponents could resist; in particular, by discrediting the press and those epistemic sources which could counter their narrative.

Part III

Capitalism, Neo-Liberalism, and Post-Modern Culture

Two Pills, One Cup: Late Capitalism and the Rise of Neomasculinity

Conrad Bongard Hamilton

"Often when we are merely enjoying ourselves, we are involved in political processes of the highest importance."
— Charles Fourier (1772 – 1837)

"All I'm offering you is the truth."
— Morpheus, *The Matrix*

The single most important cultural reference for the pickup artist (PUA) community occurs in the 1999 Wachowski siblings' film *The Matrix*. Seated in a chesterfield armchair in a dimly-lit room face-to-face with his protégé, Neo (Keanu Reeves)—whose one-note performance in the film suggests he was chosen by the Wachowskis more so to not distract attention from the film's iconic computer-generated imagery than for his acting chops—Morpheus (Laurence Fishburne) explains that Neo has to make a choice. Choose the blue pill, he states with baritone aplomb, "the story ends, you wake up in your bed and believe whatever you want to believe." Choose the red pill, and "you stay in Wonderland, and I show you how deep the rabbit hole goes."

Red Pilled Renegades

Given the ubiquity of *The Matrix* as a cultural phenom, it feels almost unnecessary to recite what follows this scene in the film, but here goes. Neo, having chosen the red pill, discovers that the world as we know it is in fact a collective simulation, created by super-intelligent arachnoid machines only slightly less dramatically expressive than Keanu Reeves himself in order to pacify humans so that their bioelectric energy can be sapped out of them. As if this weren't bad enough, he also realizes that he is in fact "the chosen one"; a messianic figure whose destiny it is to liberate humans from this artifice (though on the plus size, part of this prophesy entails him hooking up with "Trinity," a character played by Carrie Ann-Moss who—in spite of her tough exterior, which situates her clearly in the Sarah Connor/Lara Croft cross-section of taut-bodied nineties female heroines—is, basically, a nerd's fantasy).

For pickup artists—as well as for related countercultural clusters that can be broadly grouped amongst the alt-right such as men's rights activists and incels (involuntary celibates)—the red/ blue pill dichotomy is regularly employed. Its use, of course, is metaphorical—these groups have not, at least as of yet, demonstrated that what appears to be our reality is in fact fabricated by malevolent automatons bent on sapping us of our vital energies. Though their rhetoric errs very much on the side of this sort of apocalypticism. In these communities, the "blue pill" is considered synonymous with all of the spurious falsehoods propagated by groups they view as responsible for robbing men, and typically white men, of their status—feminists, liberals, "cultural Marxists," etc., the likes of whom have hijacked cultural discourse to the point where it now functions merely as a propaganda mill for their anti-masculinist views. Taking the "red pill," on the other hand, redoubles as code for dispensing with these illusions, and recognizing the "true" structure of reality; one in which male privilege is biologically embedded, and in which women, for all their hysterical, politically correct protestations, secretly long for nothing more than to be dominated by powerful, "high status" men (and who are so biologically overdetermined that their brains can be—like the binary code that flows through every square metre of the Matrix—"hacked" via the use of pickup strategies).

It goes without saying that the views of communities of men who take a scene from a tawdry sci-fi film as the basis of their message board metaphysics —made by a directorial doublet *New Yorker* film critic Anthony Lane has described as purveyors of "Pop fascism"— are, often, less than profound. But as it does shed light on our current social impasse, it will help to position this metaphor within the larger ideological constellation of these subcultures. Many of the participants in these groups, which we can refer to in general as "neomasculinist," subscribe to an anthropologically falsifiable origins story that plays out like a distorted version of Freud's fabulistic account of the death of the father in *Totem and Taboo*. In the beginning, so it goes, women were all "hypergamous"—that is to say, the majority of women reproduced with a small minority of "alpha" males, who presumably resembled Arnold Schwarzenegger in *Conan the Barbarian* (it is in fact the mainstream media who were responsible for applying the terms "alpha" and "beta"—which originate in animal ethnology—to men in their mid to late nineties; a fact that clarifies the extent to which neomasculinists represent merely the apotheosis of a far more diffuse cultural sexism). This dispensation, however, couldn't last, intolerable as it was to the swaths of "beta" males who, due to the inegalitarian sexual impulses of women, were excluded from the sexual economy. Banding together, the "beta" males—in a world-historical act of solidarity—forged the institution of monogamy, creating a form of primitive sexual communism in which erotic resources were, finally, equally distributed. But in the modern age, as Yeats wrote, the center does not hold, and today the majority of men are again finding themselves bereft of sexual opportunities—at least with the "hotter, younger, tighter" women who tend to eschew sex with all but the most desirable "chad" alphas—due to what blogger Roissy has described as the "Four Sirens" of the sexual apocalypse: "widely available contraceptives," "no-fault divorce," "women's economic independence," and "rigged feminist-inspired laws."

Men, then, must adapt. And in the absence of the immense

power and/or physical aesthetics that supposedly attract newly emancipated, fertile young women in disproportionate droves, the best way to do this is through learning the "game"—how to seduce women, through "kino" (kinesthetics, or physical escalation), "negging" (light insults intended to establish social dominance), "agree & amplify" (showing your indifference to criticisms leveled at you by complying with and rhetorically inflating them), etc. The process of learning these tricks—knowledge of which can be acquired through extensive online reading coupled with practice, or, to expedite the process, for-pay tutorials with pickup gurus—may seem strenuous. But the men forced to do it in order to enlarge their sexual appeal will be glad to know that moral comeuppance for the women who've driven these measures, in the form of "hitting the wall." "Hitting the wall" refers to the age—typically cited as around 30—at which the sex appeal of women begins to drastically decline. In effect, women have to make a choice—ride the "cock carousel" longer into their 20s/30s and pursue dalliances with "alphas" at the risk of losing their appeal as marital partners, or settle young, thereby procuring a more high status mate. What this means, in effect, is that many PUAs believe that the majority of the women they interact with—in clubs, etc.—are, so far as they've presumably decided not to marry at age 18, already in the throes of a process of self-destruction that will see them pairing off with a "beta" male "provider" once their sex appeal has sufficiently diminished that they're no longer considered sufficiently desirable to be circulated amongst "alphas." This heuristic has given rise to one of the most enduring slogans of the manosphere; one intended to poetically describe the reproductive strategy favored by most women: "alpha fux, beta bux."

The pickup communities that employ these tactics have often been hyperbolically caricatured, by outlets such as *Jezebel*, as being largely comprised of serial rapists, who justify their brutality by appealing to the intrinsic desires of women to be dominated (and there have, indeed, been a few cases of this ilk, such as that of Alex Jones and Jonas Dick). But while it's clear that adherence to strategies devised by pickup artists is hardly a pathway to a healthy relationship with the opposite sex, active members of neo masculinist communities almost universally eschew overt sexual violence, likely because it would undermine their modus operandi of acquiring approval from women (though less egregious forms of sexual violence and/or harassment are often viewed favorably). Ironically, the most dangerous members of neomasculinist communities are often those who *reject* the perverse self-help doctrines that neomasculinists so often peddle, concluding that if the world is as bad as they say it is, learning pickup tips or advocating for men's rights online isn't eligible to change it. There's a word for this—taking the "black pill," which refers to embracing a nihilism that leads either to totalizing apathy or its obverse, spectacular violence. Associated with the "incel" wing of the neomasculinist movement, in the past few years this tendency has turned homicidal, as both Eliot Rodger in San Diego in 2014 and Alex Minassian in Toronto in 2018 planned and executed attacks that left six and ten dead respectively, and that were intended above all as revenge against the archetypally beautiful "stacys" who had rejected them (as well as an incitement for others to join in an "incel rebellion" intended to dislodge the ostensibly dominant sexual coalition of alpha males and hypergamic harlots). In both cases, the agencies involved in investigating the killers, while ever quick to label attacks committed by persons of Muslim origin as terroristic, concluded that the shooters had acted not out of fidelity to groups beholden to radical ideas but as (mentally disturbed) individuals.

The Feminist Fork

Just how did we get to this point? Ironically, while the American and Canadian governments were hasty to conclude that neither Rodger or Minassian were fundamentally motivated by their identification with the radical wings of groups dedicated to the promulgation of organized misogyny, these same groups have been appealing to identity as the bedrock of their views for some years now. Not that it was always this way. In 2005, journalist Neil Strauss published *The Game: Penetrating the Secret Society of Pickup Artists*, a book that serves as a snapshot of the pickup artist community when it was, while often disturbingly sexist, largely comprised of disaffected young men swapping tips on how to meet and inveigle young women rather than plotting the destruction of the liberal order. Strauss's book was a hit, and while it was never intended as an advert for pickup artist communities it ended up arguably leading to their expansion, as well as to the contribution of the term "negging" to the popular vocabulary (and raising a serious question about the complicit character of even seemingly critical representation that can't be addressed here). But in the years between the publication of Strauss's text—which even in its time was guilty of glossing over some of the unsavory aspects of the pickup community, resulting in glamorized presentation—and the Rodger attack of 2014, something happened. Bloggers such as Roissy and Roosh V. (the former of whom has stated that while he sympathizes with white nationalists he feels they're not sexist enough) while once largely devoted to disseminating tips on how men could get ahead with women *as individuals*, instead underwent a change in which they began to speak more and more in terms of identity—white/European, male, or, both. Today, looking over the websites curated by pickup artists, it is not uncommon to find that over half the articles published deal with subjects that, to the layman, would seem strangely unrelated to picking up women—adulatory assessments of the foreign policy decisions of fellow "alpha" Donald Trump, commentaries on the neomasculinist themes in *The Iliad*, etc. Broadly speaking, this shift corresponds with what Matthew McManus has described as "postmodern conservatism," or the tendency for the right in our time to communicate through the prism of identity, turning Burke's scepticism of the Enlightenment into a topsy-turvy vertigo of conspiracy that, to a large degree, views truth as a weapon to be wielded in a larger battle between social factions.

Of course, there is a spectrum, and not all neomasculinist clusters are the same. But if such a spectrum runs approximately left to right from pickup artists to men's rights activists to incels, we should note that the overarching trend over the course of the past few years has been to the right, as well as towards a correspondingly greater degree of politicization that mirrors the radicalization of society at large in the decade after the financial crisis of 2007-08 (the same period, incidentally, in which Roosh V. and Roissy started blogging). One way to grasp this change is through the work of Marxist sociologist Pierre Bourdieu. In his seminal 1979 tome *Distinction: A Social Critique of the Judgement of Taste,* Bourdieu describes how standards of beauty are normally constructed in such a way as to favor the upper class. But through individual effort, or due to the unpredictable distribution of hereditary traits, members of lower social classes are frequently able to overcome these obstacles, achieving a level of beauty/presentation that greatly aids their allocation of cultural capital. Early on, in the wave of interest that was caused by Strauss's book and the ensuing media coverage it received, pickup artists were predominantly concerned with a kind of *social transcendence* that can easily be considered in line with Bourdieu's critique, even if Bourdieu is predominantly concerned with women. For three decades after the publication of *Distinction,* times had changed—the rapid leaps forward made by women in the West on fronts both economic and social meant that, more than at any time in recent history, women were free to make decisions about sexual partners more dictated by erotic desire than socioeconomic necessity. Into this field stepped pickup artists, young men who, while often "losers" when judged in terms of their substantive accomplishments, understood that they could sleep with women well above their normative "standard" by changing their presentational styles and, sometimes, appearances (there continues to be a strong connection between pickup culture and bodybuilding culture, though the importance assigned to it depends a great deal on the position one adopts within the manosphere regarding how visually guided the romantic decisions of women are).

In this phase, pickup artists were, while known for their annoying conduct particularly in the golden age of the "neg" in the mid-to-late 2000s, not deeply invested in lofty "political" topics (girls *don't like politics*, after all). But after 2007-08, when Western countries suffered widespread job losses that disproportionately affected men so far as they were most widespread in the industrial sector, a gradual if palpable transformation began to take place in the manosphere. Frustrated by the increasing relative economic ascent of women, and conscious of the void of moral authority opened by the discreditation of the previous policy approaches of western governments, pickup artists began to conclude that, up to this point, they'd been playing a *loser's game*. Learning how to proposition women while in the grocery store, or studying online grooming tips, might help you get laid. But in the absence of dramatic political change, it was unlikely to reverse the fundamental situation—one in which women appeared to be set to gain ground against men for the foreseeable future. In 1953, Roosh V. describes in a 2013 post for the website *Return of Kings*, a man was able to acquire a partner simply by having a good job. But today, he would have almost "no value" for women, as men need to put in "obscene amounts of work and be a masculine caricature to get basic sex." And by 2073, according to a highly scientific venn diagram that accompanies the piece, the only way to sleep with an attractive woman will be through a combination of "daily spam approaching," "fame," and "steroids." Moreover, some articles during this period directly blamed women—and, in some cases, minorities—with being responsible for unemployment rates, so far as their being in the workforce, it was theorized, had squeezed out large amounts of deserving (white) men.

Alpha God, Golden Dawn

In the context of this widespread radicalization—one that was already blurring the line between "pickup artist" and "men's rights activist" to the point where the two labels were becoming increasingly synonymous—it's difficult to understate the importance of Donald Trump's arrival on the political stage. The Donald. The God Emperor. The ZFG (zero fucks giving) alpha Golden Don sent by the forces of political destiny to foil the shot of the "bitterbitch femcunt" Hillary Clinton, undermining the liberal establishment and thus preventing the catastrophic possibility of a female President. Trump, like pickup artists themselves, had a knack for positioning himself as a crusader against the disingenuousness of the liberal class; parlaying public mistrust of the government on a range of key issues into spectacularly exaggerated claims that had the ring of truth-telling, or at least delicious perversity. You can see it in the clip of the 2016 campaign rally in Florida where he makes the declaration that "Obama invented ISIS": the way Trump, Iago-like and in sync with his audience, makes every word and awkward gesture a build-up to an impending act of violence against the political status quo. "I meant that Obama founded ISIS, literally," he would later clarify—and indeed, there is partial truth amidst this cacophony. Both a loser and a winner at the same time—something that allowed him to be both relatable and a phantasmic model for PUAs—Trump also had a knack for transgressing the boundaries of women, though, as with politics, he was able to go further than most PUAs in this respect due to his immense wealth and power. "I moved on her like a bitch," he describes of his failed efforts to aggressively seduce a married woman in the vulgar recording of his conversation between himself and Billy Bush—one in which he essentially confesses to sexual assault. But while Trump "couldn't get there" with the woman in question, whom he describes as having "changed her look" later by getting "big phony tits," he could with PUAs. As it turns out, they'd also change their look, going from a community that, while already flirting heavily with political topics, afterward became in large part a vessel for pro-Trump propaganda, joining with a loose coalition of alt-right groups that had emerged from the septic annals of Reddit subforums and white nationalist Word Presses to become a bona fide political force during the 2016 election.

To say that Trump profits due to his inveighing against the liberal status quo is not, it should be said, an excuse for assuming that that liberal status quo is without its own problems. Slovenian philosopher Slavoj Žižek has observed of Jordan Peterson—a man whose psychoanalytically grounded call for a restoration of masculine values has done much to validate the views of the manosphere intellectually in the same way that Trump validated them politically—that his appeal to "(partial) factual truth" is rendered compelling only when situated in comparison to a "politically correct" liberal left that views dissimulation as necessary to the maintenance of political order. To anyone who's had exposure to the way the more sophisticated neomasculinists form their arguments, Peterson's approach will seem immediately familiar: identify a social problem, often with a high degree of acuity, then—in lieu of a meaningful sociological analysis—propose as a solution *the thing that caused the problem in the first place*. Not enough women in certain sectors of the workforce? Maybe that's just because women are intrinsically different, and we should probably drop this demagogic push for equality altogether ha ha ha right? Similarly, many of the views neomasculinists espouse are, in fact, true at the level of social description—it's hard to deny, for instance, that normative male-female flirtation often involves the simulation of a fantasy of masculine dominance. But for neomasculinists, the ongoing complicity of women with patriarchal values does not attest to the trenchant nature of oppression but rather to the biological inevitability of their desire to be overpowered—a proclivity made apparent by the way that their calls for greater equality are in fact subconsciously aiding the creation of an even more sinister hypergamic order.

Conclusion

Just how should the left respond to this? In arguably the finest article ever written on neomasculinists, "Does anyone have the right to sex?," Amia Srinivasan makes the point that the left, in large part, lacks the capacity to adequately respond to the generalized social anxieties that birthed the incel killers. This incapacity, she claims, owes largely to the way that the pro-sex feminism of the 1980s, inaugurated by thinkers such as Ellen Willis, helped facilitate a culture where "sex is no longer morally problematic or unproblematic: it is instead merely wanted or unwanted." This fetishization of consent finds its practical expression on Tinder; an application that—with its focus on qualifying or disqualifying partners on reflexive visual grounds—reinforces the body fascisms that so frequently guide romantic decision-making. Such a depressingly myopic and contractual vision of sexual engagement contrasts, in Srinivasan's view, with a current of thought stretching from utopian socialist Charles Fourier, who advocated the idea of an ungendered "sexual minimum" through to the feminists who presaged Willis, many of whom were deeply concerned with the cultivation of a just sexual order—and who would've been unlikely, so it goes, to compare sexual relations with sharing a sandwich. And while unmentioned by Srinivasan, we can also add Marx and Engels to the list of thinkers who shared this concern, with Marx's

Fourieresque comments in *The Communist Manifesto* on the need for the overturning of bourgeois marriage and the establishment of a "community of women" predicting Engels's later study in *The Origin of Family, Private Property, and the State* of the kinship structures put forth by Lewis Henry Morgan.

Srinivasan's call for the left to pose serious questions regarding our sexual dispensation is a noble one. Though if her article has one fault, it's that—when she provides examples of what this would mean—she seems rather *timid.* Certainly, the examples she gives—of individuals who are denied sexual access on the basis of race, weight, or linguistic proficiency—are important. But these inequalities have also already been partly co-opted by liberal capitalist society, with the hiring of plus-sized models and racially diverse film ingénues regularly lauded on *Ellen* or in liberal think pieces. The word "partly" is used here deliberately, since there is clearly much more to do on the front of physical representation. What is clear, however, is that, until the left is able to think the correlation between the economy and sexual choice, the manosphere will continue to have recourse to a perverted crypto-Marxist narrative in which the elevation of disenfranchised groups is seen as a *disguise* for the disenfranchisement being widely affected by elites. Nor is it clear that the quasi-identitarian concerns Srinivasan raises can be addressed without such a critique. How can one truly overturn the sexual prejudice directed towards persons of color, for instance, without viewing it as a reflection of the economics of (neo) colonialism?

Understanding the relationship between the economy and sexual choice, of course, does not mean entertaining the demand made by neomasculinists that they be given access to swaths of stereotypically sexy, "younger, hotter, tighter" women. But it does mean comprehending that our neoliberal economic order has created clear winners and losers when it comes to sex—and that the commendable strides made in the field of women's rights have engendered a great deal of confusion for men and women alike (as well as everyone else). Commenting on the scene in which Neo is offered the blue pill or the red pill in his film *The Pervert's Guide to Ideology*, Žižek states that what is needed is not one pill or the other but rather a "third pill [...] that would enable me to perceive not the reality behind the illusion, but the reality in illusion itself." By naturalizing the injustices that permeate our social dispensation, neomasculinists—while capable of identifying social contradictions—occlude the possibility of resolving them. Many of them may be beyond turning. But by exposing how their misogyny so often conceals an underlying animus with capitalist patriarchy itself, it will hopefully be possible to prevent more men from joining their ranks.

Neoliberalism, Technology and the Creation of Postmodern Culture

Matt McManus

Introduction

The emergence of post-modern conservatism, while perhaps surprising to some, is in fact the consequence of very tangible and long term trends across global society. This is because post-modernism is not first and foremost an intellectual movement, though its inner dynamics were first consciously or unconsciously understood and expressed by intellectuals and artists. Post-modernism is a cultural phenomenon wherein formerly objective epistemological, aesthetic and moral standards for making judgments "melt into air" to use Marx's famous expression. What replaces these "objective" standards is complex. For proponents of post-modernism, the collapse of these standards opens new horizons for human creativity and the reevaluation of architectonic concepts such as the self, history, and power. I do not deny that such possibilities are indeed latent within post-modern culture, and many great artists and intellectuals have engaged in just such creative endeavors. However, post-modern culture can also produce less emancipatory effects. With the effacement of previous standards for judgment, many paradoxically turn to subjective identity as a source of stability and normative authority in an increasingly unmoored world.

Post-Modern Culture and Neoliberalism

I believe David Harvey is right to argue that post-modern culture emerges as a result of the economic, technological, and structural transformations brought about by neo-liberalism. Marx observed long ago that under capitalist conditions "all that is solid melts into air." I argue that in neo-liberal post-modern culture, this has taken place with accelerating speed and reach. Firstly, capitalist transformations have increasingly brought about growing social fragmentation and alienation as the economy becomes ever more globalized, resulting in greater labor mobility, transforming working conditions, and increasing inequality. Secondly, technological advancements have brought about a hyperreal environment where neo-liberal subjects who feel alienated from these economic transformations increasingly inhabit restricted and highly partisan communication bubbles. The result of this is a growing distrust of alternative political viewpoints and the epistemic and moral foundations upon which they rest. This leads to an even greater sense of social fragmentation, amplified by concerns that internal enemies are responsible for the woes of alienated neo-liberal subjects. Finally, there is growing anxiety about the structural inability of the state apparatus to deal with these transformations, which leads to an authoritarian push to seize political power in order to put a halt to them. I will discuss the first two trends in this section, and the final one in the next.

Post-modern culture emerges in a neoliberal context for a variety of reasons. It is distinct from post-modern philosophy—in all its variety and complexity—as constituting a specific ideological approach to claims about knowledge and politics. Neoliberal economic and political policies have oriented society towards specific conceptions of individualism that detached subjects from their ethnic and cultural identities where these were antithetical to the imperatives of global capitalism. Individual neoliberal subjects were constituted to think of themselves as consumers whose primary motivation was making decisions about what commodities to acquire and how to engage in the economy as market actors looking after their self-interest. From the standpoint of neoliberal ideology, this was to be emancipatory since ethnic and cultural barriers to the pursuit of consumption and self-interest were dissolved.

The actual consequence over the long run was to gradually dissolve the shared ethnic and cultural identities which provided individuals with the joint frameworks needed to make comparatively "objective" assessments about knowledge and politics as determined by the hermeneutics of that tradition. This increasingly led individuals to feelings of atomistic detachment from the world, generating the sense of social loneliness and isolation which is often a prerequisite for the emergence of totalitarianism. This was coupled with the rising inequality and economic instability generated by neo-liberal capitalism, best represented in the Great Recession of 2008 where the rich got richer and the poor were screwed. This generated a large segment of the population that was simultaneously less attached to the ideal of their being and their objective system of knowledge and way of going about politics, increasingly isolated and alone, and willing to blame vague omnipresent elite figures for these developments. The consequence of this was to attract many people to a reactionary politics which emphasized a return to traditional identity and its values, the destruction of the elites responsible for undermining it, while retaining the neoliberal skepticism about "objective" truths which were barriers to the pursuit of one's interest, now interpreted collectively.

Postmodern Culture and Technological Transformations

This brings me to my second point about the impact of technological transformations in a neoliberal context. The early years of the 21st century were marked by an explosion of new digital technologies and media. The projected social impact of these technologies was aligned with neoliberal ideology. New technologies would bring about the dissolution of ethnic and cultural barriers to dialogue, and thus the consumption of commodities from across the globe. This would in turn generate more understanding, tolerance as filtered via neoliberal understandings of rights, and freedom for individuals to create new kinds of identity. In some circumstances this has indeed been the case. New technologies have brought about dialectical transformations in society with both positive and negative characteristics.

We are now witnessing the negative consequence of these transformations. New technologies allowed reactionary and lonely individuals to increasingly coordinate with one another in the hyperreal medium of the internet. 4Chan, *Breitbart*, and the *Daily Stormer* rose to prominence as communication bubbles in which individuals were constantly exposed to narratives about how their given identity was under attack by liberal and multi-cultural elites who used "objectivity" and knowledge to dissolve the values of traditional identities. Constantly exposed to these digitally articulated narratives, and disconnected from the rest of the world by the imperatives of neo-liberal economics and policies, people increasingly adopted what Marcuse characterized as a "one dimensional" attitude towards the world. Seeking to reclaim space for the ethnic and cultural identities they felt had been lost, they also no longer had the ability to even recognize other such identities who also operated in neo-liberal society. Where they did recognize them, it was through the lens of a hermeneutics of suspicion rather than dialogue. This led to growing calls to move out of the digital realm back to the concrete realm of real politics. Reactionaries organized around a given identity and sought to push its understanding of truth and politics against those who argued for a different identity and affiliated values. To do this they needed to seize control of the state apparatus, still the "best" tool available to push back against social transformation and reassert the power of traditional identities and their beliefs.

Conclusion: The Emergence of Post-Modern Conservativism as a Political Movement

Reactionaries operating in post-modern neoliberal cultures and empowered by technology often given their ambitions a mythic dimension; saving Western civilization, preventing "white genocide," making America "great again" and so on. I believe these mythologized politics are deployed by reactionaries to push back against the postmodern culture of neoliberal "last men" and their elite, multicultural allies who are responsible for the loneliness and meaninglessness of neoliberal society. The wish to mobilize traditional identity as a last refuge against nihilism and meaninglessness. This results in the last tendency I associate with post-modern culture: the right wing authoritarian push to buck the erosion of the nation state and social fragmentation through advocating a malicious form of mythologized identity politics. This is what I term post-modern conservatism.

Post-Modern Conservatism and Capitalism

Matt McManus

Introduction

Conservatives have been deeply critical of what is often called postmodernism. They have associated it with identity politics, political correctness, social justice warriors, relativistic cultural Marxism and a host of other evils. For some conservatives, post-modernism signifies everything that is wrong with contemporary society. University of Toronto Professor Jordan Peterson has characterized it as "dangerous" and "radical" and dismissed important authors like Derrida as "charlatans." The National Security Council has claimed that post-modern "cultural Marxism" (whatever that means) mobilizes opposition to Donald Trump. And right wing commentator Ben Shapiro has characterized Barak Obama as the first "post-modern" President.

Moreover, conservative criticisms of postmodern thinking are not relegated to its intellectual claims. They are often directed against specific groups in society that are perceived as promulgating postmodern doctrines. Here, Jordan Peterson, now the number one selling author on Amazon, is perhaps the most articulate and comprehensive right wing critic. He criticizes postmodern theorists and scholars for corrupting the youth of the West with "nihilistic" doctrines that "rip out their ethical foundations." Most particularly, he directs his scorn against postmodernism's most pernicious product: identity politics. Taught that powerful institutions are marginalizing their identity, individuals become "hellbent" on tearing down apparently oppressive structures without appreciating the valuable service they provide. This leads to growing social fragmentation, a sense of atomistic isolation from all other individuals and groups, and destroys the "substructure of

Western Civilization" and its affiliated moral values.

There is much that could be said for defending postmodern intellectuals and theory from critics like Peterson. To my mind it is clear that they do not have a particularly robust understanding of most postmodern doctrines. But here I want to raise another, more direct criticism. Conservative critics often take various social groups who advocate for postmodernism to be responsible for social fragmentation and the alleged collapse of the Western tradition and its values. Apparently a small cabal of university professors, activists, and students, is ripping apart the "substructure" of Western civilization one Derrida citation at a time. However, these conservative criticisms all have a curious shallowness to them. By directing blame against easily targeted and reviled social groups like intellectuals (and, as we shall see, ethnic minorities), they either miss or distract from more powerful social trends which might play a far more significant role in what David Harvey calls the "production of difference" across society. I want to discuss how capitalist societies actually produce the kind of social fragmentation and atomism these conservative critics decry. Moreover, I will suggest that capital plays a fundamental role in the production of what I call "postmodern conservatism."

Capitalism and the Production of Difference

In *The Communist Manifesto,* Marx and Engels characterized capitalism as a revolutionary mode of social production where "all fixed, fast-frozen relations, with their train of ancient and venerable prejudices and opinions, are swept away, all new-formed ones become antiquated before they can ossify." In capitalist societies "all that is solid melts into air." This brilliant formulation is tantalizingly rich with insight about the impact capitalism can have in destroying old social relations, replacing them with new ones, and then in turn eliminating those. Later, Marx would elaborate on this position more concretely. In the

Grundrisse Marx claimed the production of surplus value—the value added to objects which allows them to be commodified and sold at a profit:

> "...requires the production of new consumption requires that the consumer circle within circulation expands as did the productive circle previously. Firstly quantitative expansion of existing consumption; secondly, creation of new needs by propagating existing ones in a wide circle; thirdly, production of new needs and discovery and creation of new use values."

What Marx was describing in the *Grundrisse* was nothing less than the origins of social fragmentation taking place on a global scale as capitalism grew in strength. Throughout *Capital* and other works, he elaborates on this theme. Most notably, Marx discusses how the introduction of money as the primary medium of exchange in traditionally oriented societies transforms the way individuals interact within them. From seeing one another as common members of a community, they gradually transform into egoistic and competitive consumers pursuing their own particular desires. In other words, capitalism and its mediums transformed traditional societies into those characterized by alienated modern individuals concerned only with their own identity and its private satisfactions. Moreover, since all individuals now competed with one another for position and capital, everyone became increasingly concerned with power. Where before power had been relegated to the top of the social hierarchy, in the apparently equal realm of liberal society, everyone was expected to acquire power in order to get ahead.

Years later, David Harvey developed this same idea geographically, vividly describing how capital both creates new geographies only to tear them down shortly after. Capital produces a new set of factories, service centers, and centers of production to create new moral values. This is its moment of greatest triumph; capital has successfully eliminated the old in order to market and sell the new. But what Harvey calls the "paradox" inherent in this process is that these same centers of production then post a barrier to the development of new ones designed to create new economic, and by extension, moral values. So eventually capital tears down the very geography of the old to build the new, transforming landscapes and communities as it goes.

We can develop this line of thinking even further. Capitalism must inevitably destroy old moral values in order to continuously create new ones through what Joseph Schumpeter called a process of "creative destruction." It has no use for traditional mores, since they pose a barrier to the creation of new values and the set of commodities affiliated with them. Moreover, I would claim that since we frame our identity in relation to the world around us, these new values and commodities lead to social fragmentation through the creation of new identities. Capitalism establishes new ways of being in the world, commodifies them, and gradually dissolves the social fabric that once existed in more homogenous traditional societies. Moreover, in an accelerating attempt to destroy space through time as Harvey puts it, modern global capitalism also brings the world closer together, unbalancing the traditional legitimacy and identity of the "nation" state. It does this through moving factories from the developed to the developing world to take advantage of low labor costs, relocating private assets to off shore tax free havens, or creating zones for the "free" movement of labor such as the European Union, and a host of other trends.

The power of these movements is undeniable. But as we have seen, there has been a dramatic pushback against these trends. Some of this has come from the Left. I will try to account for how capitalism precipitates the rise of what I am calling postmodern conservatism. Postmodern conservatism is highly dangerous because, rather than critically examining the root causes of social fragmentation in capitalist processes, it directs its rage against the most vulnerable in society.

Postmodern Conservatism

Post-modern conservatism draws on the philosophical heritage of those like Edmund Burke, Joseph De Maistre, Lord Devlin, Michael Oakeshott, and other conservatives. These figures located the root of social fragmentation not in capitalism and social processes, but in the ideology of liberal rationalism. They argued that liberal ideology, developed and disseminated by intellectuals fascinated with abstractions, were establishing a world where respect for traditional society and its values was being abandoned. In its place, they erected a kind of atomistic individualism, where each person was concerned to pursue their own desires without interference from others or respect for traditional values. As the late Robert Bork, Reagan's erstwhile favorite for the Supreme Court put it, progressive liberals had no interest in "particularity—respect for difference, circumstance, history, and the irreducible complexity of human beings and human societies." Against this, these classically conservative thinkers argued that individuals should respect traditional authority and be distrustful of pretentious "rational" intellectuals.

There are virtues to this intellectual tradition; for instance, Edmund Burke's staunch criticism of imperialism based on its tendency to destroy long standing cultures and traditions. However, these virtues are not shared by post-modern conservatism, which is the contemporary bastardization of this right wing intellectual tradition, vastly empowered through modern technologies such as digital media and deeply radicalized. Emerging largely on the internet in the mid-2000s, postmodern conservatism embodies what Wendy Brown characterizes as a politics of resentment. It aggressively denounces allegedly "progressive" doctrines formulated by intellectual elites who claim to have some privileged understanding that lets them arbitrate issues of facts and values with objectivity. Against this, post-modern conservatism radicalizes the positions of Burke, Oakeshott, Bork and others that the traditional "common sense" understanding of the heartland should be taken as authoritative. It is the average person in the heartland, the man on the "Clapham omnibus" to invoke Lord Devlin, whose moral values should be accepted as authoritative. Not because his values are demonstrably more valid. Postmodern conservatism, with its reverence for "alternative facts," its dismissal of different opinions as "fake news," and its distrust of intellectuals, has shown little concern for epistemic validity. Postmodern conservatives want their values accepted because that is what tradition dictates and what most "regular" people value (though apparently not enough to win a majority of votes in the United States).

Conclusion: The Roots of Postmodern Conservatism in Capitalist Processes

This is in part what makes postmodern conservatism so dangerous. Postmodern conservatism blames unpopular "elite" groups like intellectual and marginalized communities such as LGBTQ groups and ethnic minorities drawn to developed countries with the promise of jobs for the fragmentation of society. In practice, this means that post-modern conservatives have mobilized ethnic identity to push for a retrenchment of tradition, and its affiliated moral values, against the demands of both liberals who believe in objective truth and post-modern leftists who want a more pluralistic society. The irony here being, of course, that postmodern conservatives have developed their own form of identity politics. Postmodern conservatives such as Donald Trump, Marine Le Pen, or "illiberal" democrats such as Janos Ader of Hungary, have directed the outrage produced by social fragmentation against vulnerable identities who allegedly don't belong. Against the power of globalizing capitalist trends, they have demanded a return to a kind of state-oriented corporatism in which national capital is insulated from global competition by putting restrictions on competition, foreign goods, and the "free" movement of labor through immigration. This, combined with repressive domestic policies clamping down on progressive groups and "alien" identities, is meant to abet social fragmentation and help postmodern conservatives feel great again.

Postmodern conservatives have failed to see that capitalism itself is the greatest source of social fragmentation and value creation in the world. The attempts to insulate national capital from globalization, even if successful, cannot stop this trend. It is inherent in the nature of capital to revolutionize society in a manner conducive to accumulation through the creation of new moral values and the destruction of the old. Moreover, postmodern conservatives fail to see that they themselves are the product of such trends. Indeed, as David Harvey, Wendy Brown and others have observed, the modern fixation of identity and the emphasis on identity politics is itself partly the product of capitalism. Through establishing a society in which alienated individuals are seen as responsible for pursuing their private pleasure in competition with others, the political mobilization of identity can become a locus for pursuing social power. In some cases this can be an extraordinarily progressive effect, for instance when historically marginalized groups push for an equal share of the pie. However, in the case of postmodern conservatives, capitalism, combined with new digital technologies, has wrought a cabal of truth denying nationalists aggressively pushing for the retrenchment of their traditional identity, values, authority. These are the same values and positions of authority which capital itself helped dissolve while maintaining the basic hierarchy integral to capitalism.

Trump's Trade War Vanity: Post-Modern Populism and the Economy

Matt McManus

Introduction

In early 2018 Donald Trump slapped tariffs on a vast array of products coming from America's allies including: Europe, Mexico, and of course, Canada. This came months after he had initially flirted with starting a trade war, declaring that they are easy to win and therefore in America's best interest. Things got considerably worse at the G7 summit where Trump insulted Prime Minister Trudeau for holding a press conference characterizing the American tariffs as "unfair" and threatened to slap more on the Canadian auto-industry.

Trump's protectionist assault on America's friends was immediately decried for being both economically unsound and unnecessarily weakening important alliances. Chief Executive of the Chamber of Commerce Tom Donohue estimated that up to 2.6 million jobs may be lost in the United States alone. Justin Trudeau, joining a growing chorus of international leaders, indicated that Canada would impose retaliatory tariffs on end-use products valued at up to $16.8 billion. Germany's Angela Merkel threatened that the European Union would retaliate in a "firm and united" way against the "illegal" tariffs. And so on.

Why Free Trade?

Given the immediate and extraordinarily negative reception and impact of the tariffs one might wonder why Trump imposed them. Part of the answer seems to be that he understands trade—and pretty much everything else—as a zero sum game where one person's gain is another's loss. So the fact that Canada allegedly runs a "trade surplus" against the United States is mysteriously interpreted as clear evidence that Canadians are screwing America over. But this line of reasoning runs counter both to age old economic wisdom and the evidence at hand. Ever since David Ricardo first formulated the idea of comparative advantage in the 19th century, most economists regard free international trade as a mutually beneficial activity. This is because it allows countries to specialize and refine their production techniques, offers consumers and firms access to cheaper and potentially higher quality goods, and increases the amount of wealth generated over all. The NAFTA agreement was theoretically supposed to bring about just these benefits. While NAFTA has always been an imperfect agreement imperfectly enforced, most experts believe it was doing just that. By some measures, NAFTA quadrupled trade between 1993 and 2017, lowered prices on a large number of goods, and created many new jobs, including 5 million in the US alone.

The Dangers of Right Wing Populism

So why then is Trump so hostile to permitting free trade with America's traditional allies? I think the answer runs deeper than just his unusual interpretation of economics and economic data. When one looks at Trump's rhetoric around the tariffs, it is low on precision and examples but very high in resentment and a sense of victimization. Trump has claimed that Canada and America's other allies are making chumps of the United States, getting rich off of one-sided trade deals while American workers and industries suffer. This narrative of victimhood is consistent with Trump's campaign invectives about how other countries were now "laughing" at the United States, and how no one respected America's strength anymore. Of course, this was subsequently followed by calls for people to vote for him, since Trump alone could make America great again and force the world to respect it.

These latest tariffs and the trade war that will ensue are very consonant with this rhetoric, which is why America's allies and their leaders are increasingly characterized as "weak," "meek" and undermining American strength. This plays into the victimhood narrative and the almost Freudian desire to project strength and toughness that is so characteristic of the post-modern right wing populism we now see emerging around the globe. Right wing populists in America, Hungary, and Poland are distinctively post-modern in their dismissal of truth and appeal to narratives about victimized identities.

For Trump, the reality that America is probably the furthest thing from a put on country, and that international trade benefited everyone, is a truth to be dismissed. Like most inconvenient realities, it can be dismissed as biased "fake news" or through appeal to "alternative facts." What matters isn't the reality of the situation. It is propping up the paranoid narrative of victimhood and doing anything necessary to "appear" strong. This makes right wing populism extremely dangerous. It is not just dissolving important economic and diplomatic connections between states. It is dissolving our social capacity to determine what is real and what is not.

Why the Right Wing Fight Against Cultural Nihilism is Meaningless: Post-Modern Conservatism as a Capitalist Product

Matt McManus

"Across Western Europe the great word is 'emancipation': emancipation from family identity, emancipation from sexual identity. After all this emancipation, what is left? Nothingness."
Bronislaw Wildstein

Introduction

A specter is haunting the West: the specter of nihilism. Conservative critics across the globe are increasingly framing themselves as pushing against a deeply nihilistic culture. This culture is characterized by self-absorbed cynicism at best and totalitarian identity politics at worst. The story of how we got here differs with each conservative account, but the broad contours are largely the same. The Enlightenment, for all its virtues, brought about a cultural shift in orientation. Individuals from formerly stable and morally upright cultures were increasingly encouraged to question every settled value; as Kant put it, to have the "courage to use (one's) own understanding." While more liberal conservatives accept this still classically liberal cultural shift, most will still claim that it led to growing skepticism about the wisdom of traditional, most notably Christian, mores. People became increasingly individualistic and concerned to pursue their own private pleasures without concern for traditional mores, leading to greater and greater social fragmentation. These cultural dynamics were made explicit in Nietzsche's epochal claim that "God is Dead!" officially inaugurating the new age of the nihilistic "last men." According to conservative critics, today we are witnessing the dark consequences of these transformations. On the one hand, we have atomized hyper-individualistic cynics who believe in nothing and pursue only their own private pleasures. On the other hand, we see the totalitarianism of identity politics and a demand to accept further social fragmentation under the benign sounding guise of promoting "toleration" of radically un-Western groups.

The Conservative Response

According to many of these conservative critics, liberal elites are leading the charge in promoting cultural nihilism. At the political level, they push for policies that will lead to greater social fragmentation and atomism, such as higher rates of immigration from non-Western countries, the acceptance of large numbers of refugees, and concerted efforts to break down gender gaps which may exist for legitimate reasons. At the cultural level, liberal elites in the media, the entertainment industry, and academia promote post-modern and relativistic philosophies which hold that all cultures are equal and must be tolerated. This encourages generations of young people to call for the dissolution of traditional morals and institutions, under the auspices of promoting greater tolerance and pluralism. For many conservative critics, these transformations have been a disaster which demands a political and cultural response.

For more liberal conservatives such as David Rubin or Nigel Farage, the solution to cultural nihilism must be a return to classical liberal, meritocratic principles implemented by a resurgent nation-state. Other critics, including illiberal democrats such as re-elected Hungarian President Viktor Orban and Polish President Andrzej Duda, have adopted soft-authoritarian practices to push against immigrants and constrain political opposition. Finally, there are those such as Canadian superstar Professor Jordan Peterson who believe the only solution is a return to the traditional mores of Christianity. As he put it in the Amazon #1 Bestseller *12 Rules for Life:*

"A long period of unfreedom—adherence to a singular interpretive structure—is necessary for the development of a free mind. Christian dogma provided that unfreedom. But the dogma is dead, at least to the modern Western mind. It perished along with God. What has emerged from behind its corpse, however—and this is an issue of central importance—is something even more dead; something that was never alive, even in the past: nihilism, as well as an equally dangerous susceptibility to new, totalizing, utopian ideas... Nietzsche for his part, posited that individual human beings would have to invent their own values in the aftermath of God's death. But this is the element of his thinking that appears weakest, psychologically: we can't invent our own values, because we cannot merely impose what we believe on our souls."

Capitalism and Cultural Nihilism

I believe these conservative critics are deeply misguided in their diagnosis of the situation. While cultural nihilism may be on the rise, the accounts of these critics are strangely idealized. For the conservative critic, cultural nihilism has its roots in the sophistical cafes and salons of Enlightenment Paris and is now propagated by insidious liberal elites who wish to destabilize Western civilization. These accounts never acknowledge the transformative impact of far more powerful social forces: most notably the emergence of capitalism and its tendency towards the creative-destruction of traditional values. This was noted by Marx more than a century and a half ago:

"Constant revolutionising of production, uninterrupted disturbance of all social conditions, everlasting uncertainty and agitation distinguish the bourgeois epoch from all earlier ones. All fixed, fast-frozen relations, with their train of ancient and venerable prejudices and opinions, are swept away, all new-formed ones become antiquated before they can ossify. All that is solid melts into air, all that is holy is profaned, and man is at last compelled to face with sober senses his real conditions of life, and his relations with his kind."

Interestingly, more insightful and balanced conservative and traditionalist communitarian critics such as Max Weber and Alasdair Macintyre have also noted the tendency of capitalism to destroy social values in order to produce a society of desire seeking individuals who feel unconstrained by traditional mores. Since the 19th century, capitalism has transformed the globe, revolutionizing the values of every society it touches. The post-modern identity politics so disdained by many conservative critics is, in many respects, the product of just this capitalist environment. As noted by David Harvey, the post-modern position that all values are contingent and socially produced is largely consonant with the belief of capitalists that new values and related needs can be manufactured, and new subjectivities based around consumption produced. Throughout this, old values are overcome as barriers to the production of the new. To give just one example invoked by Harvey, who do you think is more responsible for the sexualization of culture: a few post-modern professors authoring dense theoretical tracts, or the television and film industry looking to make a fortune?

Conclusion: Post-Modern Conservatism as a Product of Nihilistic Capitalism

Conservative critics will never successfully abet the culture of nihilism they so disdain as long as they refuse to engage in a systematic analysis and critique of capitalist society. But very few have chosen to do so. They have instead limited their attacks to the easy targets of liberal "elites" who are at most themselves the products of capitalist dynamics. This limitation is not without consequence. It has led many right wing critics to abet the emergence of nihilistic post-modern conservatism as a reaction against social fragmentation and the alleged hegemonic power of liberal "elites."

Post-modern conservativism is the product of cultural nihilism masquerading as a solution. Post-modern conservatives claim that the locus of truth and morality are homeland identities which have been marginalized by social fragmentation and the demand for more toleration of difference. They demand that the traditional morals treasured by homeland identities be restored, and a culture of tolerance replaced by one of "responsibility" for toeing the traditional line. Oftentimes these post-modern conservatives also claim to be fighting against the nihilism of trends such as cultural relativism and social fragmentation, as with President Trump's Warsaw speech calling for a defense of "Western Civilization." But this is to be accomplished by deconstructing the ideals of truth, democracy, and respect for difference that constitute the best features of that civilization. This has resulted in the erosion of institutions and norms designed to protect the most vulnerable in society.

It is possible that the ascendancy of post-modern conservatism will even swallow the still too globalized and outdated neo-liberals who increasingly cling to power. Neo-liberal icons such as David Cameron and Hilary Clinton have seen their authority melt into air under pressure by post-modern conservatives who denigrate them as progressive liberal elites of another stripe, eager to integrate more tightly into the global economy with its rootless cosmopolitans and relativistic multiculturalists. In their place, post-modern conservatives have elected illiberal strongmen who disdain the very idea of truth and wish to establish a more homogenous nationstate that will remain oriented by internal capitalist dynamics. This is an extremely worrying development that should be of concern to all.

Part IV

Right Wing Responses to Post-Modern Culture

All Good Things Must Come to an End: An Overview of "Why Liberalism Failed."

Matt McManus

Introduction

Patrick Deneen's provocative new book *Why Liberalism Failed* is attracting the kind of attention that few academic works ever see. Even more unusually, it has enjoyed positive commentary from across the political spectrum. *The National Review's* David French praised the book for making him "think" and presented an "alluring" vision of alternatives to the liberal order. The far left *Jacobin* opined that Deneen's book is the rare piece of anti-capitalist writing by a conservative that offers a "bold and seasonable" overview of liberalism's problems. The *New York Times* placed *Why Liberalism Failed* on its Book of the Times list and opined that "readers of all political stripes" could find something in the book that "rings true."

These accolades belie the fact that Deneen's book pivots around an extraordinary,almost unbelievable thesis: liberalism isn't just in a crisis, it is on its deathbed. More radically still, according to Deneen, liberalism is in the twilight of its life not because it failed, but because it has "succeeded" tremendously. This dialectical inversion is a claim worthy of Hegel or Marx, and deserves to be treated with the same seriousness. That Deneen's book has warranted such accolades testifies to the power of his argument, even if very few commentators so far have been willing to accept his very radical thesis that liberalism is on the way out. Indeed, that such an argument is even given serious attention—coming less than 30 years after Francis Fukuyama proclaimed liberalism had triumphed and brought the "end of history"—is a testament to the strange times we inhabit within post-modern liberal culture.

The Meaninglessness of Partisanship

Deneen's book is utterly unique in its steadfast unwillingness to situate itself within traditional political categories. In this age of hyper-partisan wrangling, where "liberal" is almost inevitably followed by "cuck" or "conservative" by "racist," such an approach is an invigorating breath of fresh air. Or at least it would be if Deneen's reasoning for such a position weren't so damning.

Deneen opens his book by observing that of the three great ideologies which defined the modern (now post-modern age)—fascism, communism, and liberalism—only the last and oldest remains ideologically convincing. Yet liberalism's victory over its rivals is fundamentally pyrrhic. Far from entering Fukuyama's utopian end of history, liberalism is on the ropes. And this is not the result of any given political party or movement who have mismanaged or undermined liberal society. It is not because Democrats don't care about market efficiencies, or because the British Conservatives decided to cut a few taxes and government services here and there. Indeed, to Deneen, the great political rivalries which battle for position within liberal societies are, at base, deeply superficial and not all that meaningful. Both are ultimately beholden to the same liberal reasoning, but simply emphasize different means to achieve the same ends. Conservatives believe that the free market and meritocracy is the best way to ensure a society that respects freedom and advances the human pursuit of pleasure. Progressives believe that a substantial amount of state intervention is needed to truly enable individuals to be free and pursue their sense of the good life. But on neither side of the political spectrum is the basic end of allowing freedom to pursue pleasure questioned. Only the means are contested, giving liberal political disputes an almost technical and pedantic quality to them. The "liberocrats" who ascribe such significance to differences in means don't do so because they really are significant, but precisely because they are shallow and people needed to be agitated in caring about them. And according to Deneen, none of their policy tinkering can actually evade the reality that liberalism is wracked by massive internal contradictions which will ultimately lead to its downfall.

The Origins of Liberalism in Scientific Reason

So what evidence and arguments does Deneen give to ground such an immense claim? Ultimately his empirical evidence tends to be presented in broad strokes, as perhaps it must be when trying to argue that liberalism itself has "failed." This is a serious weakness of the book, since at times his evidence borders on the anecdotal. It is also excessively focused on the United States, as most books by American political scientists tend to be. But I shall not discuss these weaknesses here because the empirical details are largely secondary to the epochal narrative Deneen—a political theorist by training—is trying to tell. The book really comes to life when discussing the ideological characteristics and consistency of liberalism.

Firstly, Deneen follows other Roman Catholic thinkers such as George Grant and Alasdair Macintyre in developing a genealogy of liberal thought that goes further back in time than usual. To Deneen the real founder of liberalism was not a proto-liberal like Thomas Hobbes or a contractarian like John Locke. J.S Mill, perhaps the quintessential liberal and sometime hero and villain to both the right (for his defense of free speech) and the left (for his distaste for traditionalism and support for women's rights) is given surprisingly short shrift.

The real founder of liberalism was Francis Bacon (1561-1626), the English philosopher of science and tutor to Hobbes. According to Deneen, Bacon made explicit a radical change brewing within Western culture at the time. Deneen observes that previous generations of political thinkers-from Aristotle to Aquinas-saw human beings as limited natural beings who were to morally and harmoniously exist within a well ordered cosmos. On this model, our moral obligations throughout life were to fulfill the role God or nature had ordained for us in a virtuous manner. With Bacon, that all changed. Nature became both an antagonist to overcome and a resource to be put to use. Nature was responsible for disease, hunger, and ultimately death. But human reason was also capable of taking its resources and applying them to overcome these varied obstacles. It did so by putting nature on the "rack" and forcing it to reveal its secrets through the application of the experimental method. For Deneen, this superficially academic shift belied an immense transformation that would eventually impact our very sense of what a human being was. We began to abandon the vision of ourselves as natural beings who were part of a harmonious and well-ordered world. Instead we existed as singular individuals who needed to deploy their reasoning powers to get ahead through acquiring as many goods as we possibly could. The most effective way to do this is through liberty, which at base Deneen conceives of as a kind of power to do whatever we wish in the pursuit of our interests with as little interference from either nature or other people as possible.

As this sense of ourselves and the demand for greater liberty to pursue our private desires became more entrenched, liberal political philosophies emerged to give it social expression. Thinkers like Hobbes and Locke came forward and argued that within the "state of nature" human beings found themselves at the mercy of the various elements. They founded political society to ensure both their political protection and to enable their freedom to pursue various forms of pleasure, and to acquire the means to do so more effectively. Hobbes and Locke both maintained that they were simply giving descriptive accounts of what human beings naturally were, and how political society was actually established. But Deneen argues that this is a gross falsehood, one that still persists to this day (think of contemporary

"Enlightenment" militants such as Richard Dawkins and Steven Pinker). Liberalism didn't describe people as they were. As its social power grew, liberalism aggressively remade them in its image.

For Deneen, this transition is both the source of liberalism's power and the roots of its inevitable decline. The scientifically minded, freedom loving, pleasure seeking individuals liberalism created transformed the social world in line with their new political imperatives. Oftentimes this had a positive impact. Liberalism annihilated many barriers to the progress of its worldview, including upending unwelcome sexual, ethnic, and racial hierarchies to a degree never before seen. It also brought about an increase in living standards by providing the political backdrop for the emergence of capitalist economics, which unleashed an industrial revolution which transforms our world to this day. And of course, in addition to annihilating its internal enemies within society, liberalism's resilience allowed it to triumph in the long battles against Fascism and Communism in the 19th and 20th centuries. So why then is liberalism doomed? Deneen gives a myriad of reasons. Here I will focus on the two reasons which are most convincing.

Why Liberalism Failed

The first reason liberalism has failed is fundamental. Deneen observes that the political promise of liberalism has always been to provide full liberty for all. But to Deneen, this is ultimately impossible. This wasn't due to some failure of liberalism to deliver, but because its own success will ultimately lead to the watering down of real civic and private freedom. As people demand more and more private liberty, they will also want more control over their environment. This will ultimately lead to the establishment of an ever growing state to provide for our needs and to protect us from our limitations. Deneen argues that even the early liberal thinkers—Jefferson, Madison, Mill—

foresaw this, which is why they often deliberately limited the democratic features which were to be incorporated into liberal political structures. Liberty for private individuals meant the freedom of citizens needed to be limited, and a new epistemic aristocracy established. In practice, this has meant that remote class of technocrats has taken charge to deliver the goods as effectively as possible. Liberal politics is characterized by voting once every few years for the representatives of various political parties who have different visions of how best to provide people with the goods needed to overcome nature and its limitations. Beyond such largely symbolic forms of political participation and freedom, liberal citizens have little actual control over what happens in their societies. This isn't a bug in liberalism. Limited political freedom is needed if liberty from the limitations imposed by nature is to be achieved as efficiently as possible.

This might make Deneen sound like some kind of small state conservative. But he is not, since the capitalist market is just as much a feature of liberal society, and therefore just as infected with fundamental tensions. This brings me to the second reason why liberalism has failed. Liberal markets—capitalism in other words—also make us more unequal and less free. This is perhaps the most shocking discussion in Deneen's book. He observes how liberalism and capitalism proceeded to efface traditional cultures and mores—about sex, gender, and virtue—which stood in the way of commodification and consumption. The societies governed by such mores were often deeply, even intolerably, illiberal. But individuals within them were also governed by minimal governments and enjoyed a sense of real equality with others. Differences in lifestyle were fairly minimal, communities often helped their members get ahead in a non-competitive environment, and many felt themselves to be part of a shared culture with deep roots in the past.

Liberalism was predicated on a very risky socio-economic gamble. Early liberals knew that such traditional cultures and mores stood in the way of market expansion, and that over time capitalization would lead to far greater economic inequality. Their gamble was both that liberal capitalism could successfully remake individuals in its own image, transforming them into competitive, isolated market actors. It would compensate for this flattening of culture and greater inequality by providing such a surfeit of goods to everyone at all ends of the economic hierarchy who would apathetically come to accept liberal capitalism. Moreover, liberal citizens would gradually cede any and all rights and power to radically change the economic system. Political institutions would legally protect corporate power—whether operated by markets or the state— and stifle any efforts at fundamental transformation that would seek to redistribute economic wealth and power. Deneen invokes the work of Tyler Cowen, in his book *Average is Over,* as a spectator of what the future might hold for a liberalism on life support. Gradually liberal society will become so fragmented that only the richest and most successful 10 per cent or so of citizens will enjoy real life opportunities and the chance of civic involvement. The remaining lower classes will be bought off with cheap videogames and idle entertainment, while all the while shutting up and accepting their place in the political and economic order.

Conclusion

Deneen's book concludes with the observation that, contrary to the claims of people like Cowen, we are not moving towards such an eternal liberal "utopia." As the worrying election of Trump and other demagogues—what I have called post-modern conservatives—indicates is that the population is turning to radical and deeply illiberal movements which will allow them to smash the current system at any cost. This has befuddled liberals on both the left and the right who secretly believed that citizens could be endlessly bought off; either with a few patchwork welfare programs, or with cheap commodities, spectator entertainment and fast food. *Why Liberalism Failed* ends with both a warning and a call for political theorists to help conceive of a new post-liberal future that retains the best features of liberalism while eschewing its fundamental problems and failures.

So is Deneen right? *Has* liberalism failed? I think in the long run nothing wrought by the hand of man lasts forever. This includes political ideologies. We have a tendency to naturalize the world as it is, and assume that things can never change. That liberalism itself was a transformative force in history that emerged a scant four centuries ago—according to Deneen at least—is often unacknowledged by those who assume it has an eternal future ahead of it. Whether it is true that liberalism has failed and is entering the winter of its life, Deneen's book is a timely rejoinder to such hubris and lack of imagination. Whether one is a liberal or not, we all should recognize that things could not go on the way they were indefinitely.

Jordan Peterson and Conservative Critiques of Modernity

Matt McManus

Introduction

Canadian university Professor Jordan Peterson made headlines when left-wing superstar Slavoj Zizek attacked him as being an alt-right supporter in the pages of *The Independent*. This is a deeply odd claim. Jordan Peterson has long described himself as something of a centrist, arguing that society needs a reasonable number of people to push for progress and an equal number to preserve traditions. That hasn't stopped him from becoming an intellectual hero to various right wing groups for his stands against using a diverse array of gender pronouns, for his fight against PC culture at the University, and his attacks on post-modernism. Despite the accolades from these groups, bordering on hagiography at points, many of these groups, strangely, seem disinterested enough in the actual content of his ideas. There is a frustrating tendency to just accept the surface of what he says—aka Jordan Peterson says post-modernism is bad, end of story—than actually probe why he makes these arguments. Here, I plan on theorizing a bit on why he has taken these right wing positions, and want to show that Peterson's analysis of modernity is flawed.

Peterson and Modernity

One of the unfair criticisms directed against Jordan Peterson by some on the far left is that he strongly supports alt-right and even racist positions. While he hasn't done everything he should to disavow support (or taking money) from some of these groups, there is little to suggest that Peterson is a closet racist. His main book *Maps of Meaning* opens with a touching, if overly sentimental, account of his interest in learning what accounts for the development of totalitarianism in society. Inspired by Jung and Nietzsche, Peterson then proceeds into an interesting review of various foundational myths in Western and other cultures. This culminates in an extensive look at the structure of Christian myth, including its treatment of evil in the figure of Satan. Peterson argues that it is Satan's pride and desire to dominate the world, regardless of the cost to its inner value, which forms the core of his evil nature. He then goes on to argue that, with the advent of secular nihilism in our scientific era, people in modern societies have gone on to react in one of two ways. Some individuals become increasingly hyper skeptical and by extension apathetic. While he doesn't single them out as such in this book, it isn't hard to connect this category of persons to the post-modern relativists Peterson now claims to despise. Other individuals become radicalized, turning to totalitarian philosophies as a way to re-establish some sense of control over the world. In *Maps of Meaning*, Peterson's main targets are reactionary groups like Fascists and Communists. Today, it also isn't hard to see him connect this category to various advocates of PC culture who want to control language and dictate what is taught and discussed.

There is an undeniable appeal to this argument, and Peterson writes in an engaging and passionate way. I think he is in part right that the advent of modernity resulted in social trends pushing people towards skeptical apathy or radicalization. I would be more sympathetic if these arguments were presented in a less self-important manner. Even in 1999, Peterson often wrote in an intensely personal way; as though he is on an epic quest to discover the roots of all social ailments. This attitude can be admirable, but also cloying. It is less noticeable in *Maps of Meaning* than it has recently become, when Peterson often speaks as though he is single -handedly fighting the most important battle of our time. This is a rather grandiose sentiment for someone whose primary target seems to be university policies, and is an unfortunate propensity on the part of many intellectuals. We are often prone to suspecting that what are ultimately largely academic battles must have some greater significance.

But this isn't my major issue with Peterson. My main problem with him is that there really isn't much that is original or all that interesting in his primary arguments anymore. Much of it has been said before. And where he tries to update these arguments by directing them at new targets—for instance post-modernism—he often doesn't seem to have a good understanding of what he is criticizing.

Conservative Critiques of Modern Life

The argument that the movement to secular modernity has resulted in either apathetic skepticism or radicalization is hardly new to conservatism. As far back as the 19th century, great critics like Max Weber were making these observations. Often they did so in a way that was deeper and more interesting than Peterson. Weber is probably the most notable. Throughout his lengthy work, Weber argues that modernity has led to what is often called the "desacralization" of the world. Where once the world was taken as a sacred and mythical place, filled with independent meaning by religious and traditional doctrines, it is now perceived as a secular and instrumental eye. We look at the world as matter in motion that can be manipulated for human needs. This has a positive upswing. Combined with the powers of modern technology and science, it means that we have been willing to transform the world to improve the quality and length of human life. The benefits of this are pretty obvious. Even a relatively poor Canadian would probably take their life in 2018 over living as an aristocrat in the 18th century,without central heat, electricity, cellphones and all the other wonders of the modern world. But Weber pointed out that this has a downside. The desacralization of the world has also meant that people no longer feel they have any deeper meaning to their lives. They feel like empty numbers governed by "specialists without soul, sensualists without heart;" replaceable cogs in the social machinery. As Weber pointed out in his *Politics as a Vocation* lectures, such people are prone to either apathetic resignation to the gloom of their temporary pleasures or radical attempts to restore some kind of deeper meaning to the world.

So far Peterson would probably agree with much of this, updating it as needed. The problem is, where Weber and other great conservative thinkers give deep and often tragic reasons for why modernity resulted in secularization and desacralization, Peterson sticks exclusively to the surface. His primary target for these trends seems to be professional. The reason people feel that their lives increasingly have little meaning is because a number of left-wing post-modern intellectuals have been spreading doctrines to that effect. This is a rather superficial analysis. It is also very self-serving, since it means that intellectuals who refuse to conform to this post-modern trend are at the forefront of saving civilization from its enemies. For any academic who has found it difficult to get students to read a 10 page article, let alone convert them into Foucault's disciples, this is a remarkable claim. It essentially makes the to and fro of academic fashion into the primary battlefield of our culture. Other intellectuals have been prone to this conceit. Heidegger is the most notable example in the last few decades. But Peterson is especially prone to thinking in these terms, and has convinced many of his followers and admirers on the right to adopt this viewpoint.

Capitalism, Technology, and the Sacred

Few great conservative thinkers have ever given in to this self-serving tendency. Part of the reason is that really probing into the roots of desacralization often means criticizing social forces many conventional conservatives happen to like. This is what a great thinker does; they challenge their followers to look closely and critically at their own prejudices. While Peterson panders to his followers by pinning blame on groups and people they already dislike, a great thinker like Weber opens up tragic spaces of choice and re-evaluation.

Take Weber for example. For Weber the collapse of tradition and mythology was brought about in no small part due to capitalism. Capitalism, with its relentless compulsion to transform the natural world into a collection of objects for exploitation, drove the creation of nihilistic ideologies where individuals gave up their conventional beliefs to become consumers. This was also the point made by Arthur Schumpeter when he talked about the "creative destruction" of capitalist forces. In the continuous need to create new values to market and profit from, capitalist forces destroyed traditional ways of life to erect new ones. Now neither Weber nor Schumpeter was anti-capitalist per se. Weber was cautious towards it, Schumpeter often wrote in praise of it. But both recognized that if one wanted the benefits of capitalism—with its vast array of new products and technologies—one had to be prepared to give up on a world that was treated as the sacred territory of God.

The same is true of technology. Heidegger was another great critic of modernity who observed that developing technologies means treating the world as meaningless "standing reserve" to be manipulated for our purposes. This applies in a modern context where digital technologies allow us to manipulate and present our identity to an immense degree, including by sticking within a fragmented communication bubble rather than going outside and interacting with others who are part of our shared culture. Each of these thinkers would probably think it was very ironic that someone like Peterson would decry the collapse of traditional values while simultaneously becoming a YouTube star pandering to ever more fragmented social groups and profiting off of their resentment.

The forces of technological and economic change are

extremely powerful and transform society in ways we often have difficulty understanding. It is much easier, and more comforting, to ascribe blame for social transformation to specific individuals and groups who are seen as single handedly moving society in a direction we do not care for. But this ascribes far too much agency to human actors and intellectual ideas.

Take post-modernism, for example. I believe it is very much a cultural epoch brought about by technological transformations in the way we interact and communicate. It is very tempting to regard technological mediums as simply a neutral tool. But technological mediums are not simply neutral, especially when it comes to communication. As the prophet of the post-modern epoch—Marshall McLuhan—put it: "The medium is the message." When we communicate through television, radio, and tweets on the internet this fundamentally changes the content we espouse and how it is received. These transformations were also well noted in Neil Postman's prophetic work *Amusing Ourselves to Death.* Postman argued that with the advent of television, modern people were gradually losing their ability to think through complex information the way they had when inhabiting a highly literate print civilization. This is because new mediums such as television were inclined to present complex issues by encapsulating it in a five minute soundbite. The immense competition for attention and views also meant that the entertainment value of the information had to be upped, increasing the temptation to give it a hyperbolic and partisan spin. This greatly empowers the partisan identity politics Peterson and others so despise.

Conclusion

My point isn't to suggest that Peterson is a bad conservative thinker per se. He isn't. When he focuses on topics he is familiar with and trained in, like the structure of myths or the psychoanalytic thought of Carl Jung, he often says engaging and interesting things. But as a political commentator he doesn't really add much to conservative discourse. Where he says something valid, it has often been said before and better. This isn't a bad thing in itself. But where he tries to update these ideas, for instance by attacking post-modern intellectuals, he is often superficial and not particularly deep. Oftentimes he is simply pandering to the prejudices of his followers. A truly great intellectual should challenge his followers, and where necessary, make them recognize where their own conceits and prejudices reinforce tendencies they claim to hate. As Kant pointed out, these moments of critical reflection are what the Enlightenment was all about. If we value our heritage, we need conservative or conservative friendly intellectuals to stop pandering to their followers and to start motivating them to be more reflective about the culpability of complex social forces—including those we may admire—in generating problems facing the modern world.

A Critique of Jordan Peterson

Matt McManus

Introduction

Since his 2016 statements in opposition to Canada's Bill C-16 Jordan Peterson has rocketed to international fame and infamy. On the right, he has been the subject of laudatory and even hagiographic praise in the pages of the *National Post* and the *National Review*. Ben Shapiro's *Daily Wire* has published a string of articles praising Peterson and dismissing his critics for publishing "dishonest, malicious crap" about him. All this furor led the *New York Times* to christen Peterson the most "influential public intellectual in the world."

On the left, criticism has been equally scathing. Tabatha Southey of *Macleans* characterized Peterson as "the stupid man's smart person." The same *New York Times* which begrudgingly acknowledged his influence called Peterson the "custodian of patriarchy." The prestigious *New York Review of Books* ran an article by Pankaj Mishra discussing the eerie proximity of many of Peterson's opinions to those of fascists and right wing mystics. And so on.

Maps of Meaning and *Twelve Rules for Life*

I find many of these often hyperbolic observations, both laudatory and damning, to be disproportionate to the actual content of Peterson's academic work and lectures. Overall he is a reasonably good academic when he writes and speaks about subjects he's familiar with. I think one's tolerance for his actual arguments depend a great deal on one's acceptance of the primarily Jungian theoretical framework he relies on. Peterson is concerned to show that the archetypal images and narratives which emerge from our unconscious mythological, literary, and religious heritage contain psychological wisdom and clues into how human beings establish meaning in our lives. I've always found Jung quite interesting, if occasionally grandiose, so I appreciate some of what Peterson says.

Peterson's first book, *Maps of Meaning*, invokes Jung, Nietzsche, and a host of other major thinkers to try and describe how and why human beings formulate their sense of life's significance. Much of this involves an in depth analysis of ancient mythology and religion. Peterson's analysis is often intriguing but involves no small bit of grandstanding. Indeed, the book includes a letter Peterson wrote to his father discussing the alleged gravity of his discoveries:

"I don't know, Dad, but I think I have discovered something that no one else has any idea about, and I'm not sure I can do it justice. Its scope is so broad that I can see only parts of it clearly at one time, and it is exceedingly difficult to set down comprehensibly in writing.... Anyways, I'm glad you and Mom are doing well."

This comes across as more than a little hyperbolic and arrogant. Indeed, Peterson is very much at home with other right wing intellectuals—notably Heidegger—who ascribed their work a tremendous social significance disproportionate to what one might expect from an academic tome on myth, psychology, and meaning. But *Maps of Meaning* does contain some interesting and occasionally even profound insights into subjects as diverse as the role of Lucifer in Christian mythology and eschatology, and even a few interesting asides on the modernized form of these archetypes in comic books and blockbuster cinema.

Peterson's second book, *12 Rules for Life*, draws on this theoretical framework but updates it with more humanizing case studies drawn from Peterson's private life, his work as a professional psychologist in Toronto, and from public history. The book is mainly designed as a self-help manual, albeit one that draws on the wide range of theoretical interests initially presented in *Maps of Meaning*. Understood that way, much of the advice Peterson offers strikes me as well intended. It certainly has proven inspiring to its audience of mostly youngish men. *12 Rules for Life* also includes some interesting asides, such as his analysis of the psychic motivations of the Columbine killers and their "religious" belief in the worthlessness of human life. Peterson is a fan of Dostoevsky, and his writing can occasionally invoke the infernal power of *Crime and Punishment* or the chapters on Ivan in *The Brothers Karamazov*.

Jordan Peterson and the Left

The major problems I have with Jordan Peterson emerge when he tries to extend his ideas into politics. Here things get rather murky. Despite having a partial undergraduate degree in Political Science from the University of Alberta, Peterson has little professional background writing or researching on politics or political theory. His academic work discussing politics largely consists of writing papers relating psychological dispositions to very broadly defined political ideologies, and scattered comments throughout his two major books. Many of his comments are passionately articulated but hyperbolic. Few are well argued.

Maps of Meaning established the theoretical binary which seems to guide Peterson's approach to politics. This is the binary between masculine order and feminine chaos, which Peterson finds archetypally represented in a number of mythological, religious and literary cultures. He believes that conservatives tend to psychologically veer towards favoring order and tradition, while the left veers towards favoring chaos and transformation. Peterson believes that societies require both tradition minded conservatives and creative progressives to remain balanced. Where they become imbalanced, as in Nazi Germany or the Soviet Union, societies become increasingly totalitarian or anarchic. Peterson argues that contemporary

Western societies have veered too far towards favoring left wing chaos, and have as a result abandoned the traditions and mores which have unconsciously guided us towards wise decisions and the establishment of an enduring civilization. Today, the leftists pushing for unbalanced chaos are "collectivist" identity politics activists guided by radical post-modern neo-Marxist philosophies.

Jordan Peterson is concerned about the ascendency of the post-modern left because he sees it as eerily reminiscent, even inspired by, the collectivist philosophy of the Soviet Union. Drawing on Aleksandr Solzhenitsyn's profoundly tragic account of Soviet atrocities in *The Gulag Archipelago,* Peterson asserts that the moral legitimacy of Marxism was forever destroyed by the mid-20th century. As a consequence, the Left no longer had a respectable philosophical framework to draw upon. As a result, it turned to post-modern neo-Marxism, which is effectively the same collectivist philosophy except now generalized beyond the class analysis characteristic of Marx's work.

Guided by post-modern neo-Marxist philosophers like Foucault and Derrida, the Left has gone beyond just criticizing class based exploitation. The Left now criticizes the impact of all forms of power; especially its impact on so called marginalized groups in society. Because power is understood very broadly, and impacts a huge number of different groups, this has meant that the Left is increasingly concerned to tear down all traditions and mores in society in its quest for "equality of outcome" across all social groups. Peterson is concerned that this even more radically "collectivist" philosophy is very dangerous and will lead to the formation of a "vast" and totalitarian bureaucracy that will oversee and police our every actions, right down to the way we address one another. This is why Peterson believes it is plausible to link a trans-rights activist with a Maoist revolutionary; the collectivist "philosophy which guides their utterances is the same" since both mobilize group identity to allegedly push for equality of outcomes while destroying classical liberal freedoms. It is also why Peterson ascribes such insidious significance to campus radicals and their attempts to shut down free speech through acts of shaming, establishing prohibitions, and even violence. Far better that these activists take some time to set their own lives in order before criticizing the world, after which they would apparently recognize the wisdom of Peterson, and those like him, who venerate our auspicious traditions and mores.

Jordan Peterson on Marxism

There are a wide number of problems with Peterson's characterization of the Left. Firstly, it is pretty clear that Peterson simply doesn't know that much about Left wing theory or activism. Take his characterizations of both Marxism and so called post-modern neo-Marxism. Peterson's decision to blame Marxist philosophy for the appalling crimes of the Soviet Union and Maoist China is deeply problematic. There is an extensive literature on the relation between the Marxism and the communist regimes, but virtually no scholar argues that either the Soviets or the Maoists were in any way faithful to Marx's initial theories. To give an example, both Lenin and Mao launched communist revolutions in poor developing countries wracked by war. This is in staunch contrast to Marx's insistence that Communism could only take root in developed states where the "means of production" were highly advanced. Or to give another example, Marx argued that global capitalism was wracked by contradictions which would eventually exacerbate economic and political crises around the globe. But Soviet Communism and Maoist China both emerged during periods when the capitalist economy was either chugging along or booming. These examples, and many others, undermine the claim that Marxist philosophy inevitably leads to the gulag and the Great Leap Forward. Peterson might contest this by arguing that the root problem is the "collectivist" and anti-traditionalist philosophy underpinning Marxism. This is a very shallow reading of Marx, who was concerned for individual freedoms and criticized capitalism for destroying traditional values. It also ascribes undue blame for the impact one's philosophy might have on others. Peterson might think that invoking Solzhenitsyn is a decisive rebuttal, but I remain unimpressed. Much as I would be if someone were to present an account of the Spanish conquest of Latin America, approved by the Pope and responsible for the deaths of 187 million people over the century, as a decisive rebuttal of Christianity as a whole. Or if someone invoked the Nazis' reverence for Nietzsche, a favorite author of Peterson, as a reason not to read the great German thinker.

But Peterson is not essentially concerned with Marxism. Peterson lazily believes Marxism is so thoroughly discredited that he is apparently above actually engaging with what Marx or intelligent Marxists like Fredric Jameson, a scathing critic of postmodernism, have actually said. Instead Peterson is concerned with what he calls postmodern neo Marxism. But is there such a thing?

Jordan Peterson on "Postmodern Neo-Marxism"

The idea that postmodernism is simply Marxism by another name would surely surprise many on the Left who regard the two as inimical to one another. Postmodernism largely emerged as a reaction against the thoroughly modernist narrative underpinning Marxist theory. It is an aesthetic and philosophical rejection of the "grand narrative" claims of individuals like Marx, who believed that there was a "science of history" which could be discerned by acute dialectical materialists. Post-modernists in the vein of Foucault and Derrida problematize the idea that one can develop such objective "sciences;" inadvertently aligning themselves with a long undercurrent of skeptics in Western thought which can be traced back to the Sophists of Ancient Athens. While Marx was certainly an influence on postmodern thinking, as he was an influence on economists, writers, and sociologists, Marxism is in no way a direct precursor to postmodernism. If anything, many Marxists are damningly critical of postmodernism in all its variants.

Why does Peterson get this so wrong? I think the answer is that he simply doesn't know much about it, or doesn't care to present a more complex narrative that would problematize his cute and hyperbolic story about the Left. During his lectures, Peterson has admitted to reading a fair bit of Foucault and struggling with Derrida, which is hardly a basis for such sweeping generalizations. These problems persist in his written work. In *12 Rules for Life*, Peterson primarily targets, indeed conflates, the Frankfurt School of Critical theory and Derrida. But he only cites a single book by one member of the Frankfurt School and largely ignores any of Derrida's substantial works. This is a deeply shallow sample of the literature that makes one wonder whether Peterson has actually read many authors in a tradition he claims to understand and vilifies. If he had, he would know that many authors in the Frankfurt school, including its contemporary proponents like Jürgen Habermas and Axel Honneth, are highly critical of post-modernism and everything it stands for.

Finally, Peterson argues that the postmodern neo-Marxists press for the destruction of all social hierarchies and the attainment of full equality-equality of outcomes rather than opportunity-for all marginalized groups. He worries that this will lead to the establishment of a totalitarian bureaucracy. It is hard to even argue against this since so few-if any-Leftists actually argue that all hierarchies should be destroyed and outcomes equalized for all. Perhaps he is thinking of G.A Cohen or Jacques Rancierre, who occasionally flirted with such hyper-egalitarian claims. But neither are post-modernist thinkers, nor have their more extreme arguments gained much currency.

Conclusion

When you boil it down, I think that most of Peterson's distaste for the left stems from distaste for its activists and style rather than anything substantial. I also think this accounts for much of his popularity on the right, which has long held that academia and left wing activism suppress the expression of conservative views. Whether his characterization of the Left's positions is right or not, many people "feel" the same way about progressive activists as Jordan Peterson, and so just assume he must be correct in his characterization.

I have some sympathy with his criticisms of left wing activism, as indeed do other leftist thinkers such as Slavoj Zizek. Indeed, many contemporary left wing thinkers have both abandoned post-modernism and are highly critical of political correctness, though Peterson seems unaware of this. But a distaste for identity politics-which has been around in liberal societies since at least the Abolitionist movement and in many ways is a thoroughly liberal form of activism-and political correctness is not a license to engage in shallow generalizations about one's political opponents. Peterson can be an intelligent and knowing scholar when he knows what he is talking about and reigns in his worst impulses. But he cheapens intellectual discourse when he deals with caricatures and hyperbole rather than really engaging the ideas of his political opponents.

A Critique of Jordan Peterson-Part II

Matt McManus

Introduction

Earlier in this book, I argued that much of the hyperbole surrounding Peterson, both positive and negative, was overstated. I maintained that he was a talented scholar when he focused on his areas of expertise; namely psychology, and its association with mythology, religion, and literature. This is reflected in the overall quality of his magnum opus, *Maps of Meaning*. While an overambitious and occasionally grandiose book, it contained many interesting insights into how human beings formulate meaning for their lives. I also observed that Peterson's recent bestseller, *12 Rules for Life: An Antidote to Chaos*, contained a significant amount of good life advice that seemed to be inspiring to its audience of mostly young men.

However, I also observed that Peterson ran into significant trouble when he stepped outside of his area of expertise to try and comment on politics. I mainly focused on the problems with Peterson's criticism of Left wing philosophy and activism. I observed that he did not seem to understand, or know very much about, what he set out to criticize. In particular, Peterson offered very shallow arguments against so called "post-modern neo-Marxism." I concluded by maintaining that the locus of Peterson's appeal as a critic of the Left was that many people *felt* the same way he did about left wing activism. They therefore assumed that he was offering salient criticisms of the philosophy allegedly underpinning this activism. I do not believe this to be the case, which is unfortunate since Peterson has the capacity to be a good scholar when he tries. This makes his unwillingness to engage with the left in any substantive and fair way disappointing.

Here, I am going to conclude my critique of his work by dealing with the more constructive dimension of Peterson's political thought. This consists of his support for "classical liberalism," meritocracy, and Judeo-Christian tradition. While Peterson is on intellectually more firm ground when invoking these tropes to offer psychological advice, his positions become confusing and even self-contradictory when generalized to the level of politics.

Agency, Hierarchy, and Setting One's House in Order

Far into *Maps of Meaning* Jordan Peterson comments on the archetype of the "decadent:" a person who shirks responsibility for their life and assumes that everything which happens to them is the product of social circumstance and bad luck. He characterizes this person, willing to blame others for their lot, as psychologically fueled by resentment and jealousy towards those who have more than they do. Peterson sees this archetype embodied most maliciously in the figure of the Soviet Communists, who engaged in brutal violence to take from those they viewed as privileged and therefore responsible for their poorer lot in life. Here I will quote Peterson at length since this passage neatly summarizes his political position:

"For example, when I am faced with a frustrating situation I do not ask myself what I am going to do about it. I ask myself who is responsible for it – and I am always ready to conclude that if the other person were to act properly then the problem would not exist. What is evil about that, you ask? Obviously if I am determined to overlook my own part in the failure to resolve my own frustrations, if I am determined to find a scapegoat for my problems, then I am just a stone's throw away from the mentality that was responsible for Hitler's final solution, or for the Spanish inquisition, or for Lenin's cultural cleansing. What was it you told me when I complained about the flaws in capitalism, about the fact that so many people take advantage of the capitalist system? Something like 'the fact that people go on consolidating their financial position ad nauseum is another problem, but it is no reason to conclude that there is anything virtuous in refusing to even try to consolidate one's position in the first place.' But it is so much easier to crown one's cowardice and laziness with the accolade of virtue."

Peterson's argument effectively seems to be that demands for a redistribution of goods and resources are predicated first and foremost on the resentment of some individuals towards those who appear better off. Peterson is therefore highly suspicious of arguments for redistribution because he believes that the underlying psychological motivation is not ultimately to make individuals better off. It is to seek revenge against those who have worked hard and achieved more in life. This psychological interpretation of individuals who push for a more egalitarian distribution of goods and resources as proto-totalitarians is also reflected in Peterson's biographical account of becoming disillusioned with his early socialism. He recounts reading *The Road to Wigan Pier* and agreeing with George Orwell's observation that many socialists do not care a whit for the poor. They only hated the rich. This super hero origin story is recounted in both *Maps of Meaning* and *12 Rules for Life*, highlighting the importance of this insight for Peterson's political inclinations. Interestingly, the primary purpose of *The Road to Wigan Pier*, namely, to present Orwell's staunch defense of socialism, is ignored by Peterson in his first book and quickly brushed past in the second.

Peterson's belief that a desire for a more egalitarian distribution of goods and resources is predicated on dangerous resentment seems to be the basis for his more concrete political positions on hierarchy and distributive justice. These are presented, in a rather scattered way, throughout his two books and many lectures and interviews. Peterson believes that, rather than blaming others or social institutions for our failings, individuals should look to their own efforts. These political beliefs are often linked with his psychological injunctions to "set your house in perfect order before you criticize the world" and to "stand up straight with your shoulders back." Rather than blaming capitalism for being poor, or patriarchy for not being admitted into a STEM program, individuals should apolitically focus on what they can to do to better their lot.

At times, Peterson connects this to arguments about the natural inevitability of hierarchy, and the traditional Judeo-Christian virtues of a meritocracy. Chapter One of *12 Rules for Life* opens with a now (in)famous discussion of how even simple lobsters, our genetic relatives, organize themselves into hierarchies based on attributes associated with physical and sexual dominance. Throughout *12 Rules for Life*, Peterson suggests that the possession of analogous attributes in humans, such as higher intelligence or competitive/aggressive drives, will inevitably lead us to organize into similar hierarchies. Sometimes Peterson is fatalistic about this, claiming that we must simply accept it as the way we naturally are. As he sometimes puts it: "life is suffering: and "unfair." Some people will be on top, and others will not. Other times Peterson invokes the aforementioned meritocratic virtues to suggest that hierarchy is not just inevitable, but desirable. This suggests that individuals should take responsibility for developing the attributes necessary to wind up at the top of the pecking order.

In combination, Peterson rather mysteriously seems to believe that these injunctions reflect an individualism consistent with a grab bag of what is best in the Western-and other- traditions. At times he aligns it with the individualism of Judeo-Christian doctrine, at other times with "classical liberal" principles. Sometimes he'll invoke Buddhist and Daoist symbology and mythology to buttress the claim that life can be unfair. This erudition is impressive, but also extremely confusing. Peterson links doctrines that are not entirely consonant-even in contradiction-with one another. Take the example of liberalism and Judeo-Christian doctrine. Liberalism from Hobbes onwards largely emerged as a reaction against traditional Christian doctrine. Liberals such as Locke, Voltaire and others argued that individuals should reason for themselves, be suspicious of tradition, and look to their private happiness. This is in stark contrast to Christian philosophers, such as the Thomists, who argued that reason was the handmaiden of faith, that religious traditions going back to Abraham should be venerated, and that pursuing the "good" was more important than private satisfaction. Unfortunately this is just the first instance where confusion sets in.

Psychological Advice and Political Theory

It is very difficult to know how to interpret Peterson's political positions because they are not presented in a transparent and precise manner. As mentioned, they are mostly presented in association with psychological advice offered to hypothetical individuals in need of guidance and wisdom. Now there is nothing wrong with this in itself, and the criteria for what constitutes good psychological advice at any one time is significantly different from what constitutes a consistent and defensible political outlook. But problems arise when Peterson tries to generalize from this advice to defend a certain type of politics.

Take Peterson's comments about hierarchy. At points, he invokes the idea of natural hierarchy to dismiss the alleged claims of left wing thinkers that hierarchies are entirely the product of unjust social institutions like global capitalism. It is difficult to actually make heads or tails on what this is meant to suggest. Firstly, I am unaware of anyone, even on the far left, who argues that all hierarchies are inherently unjust and must be eliminated. Even proponents of anarchism maintain that certain hierarchies, for instance speaking order in public meetings, must be maintained to ensure social stability. And the feminist activists who want more female CEOs running Fortune 500 companies are certainly not anti-hierarchy. No one denies either that hierarchy is a feature of human life or that it is needed in some circumstances. Debates about hierarchy aren't debates about whether any hierarchies should exist. They are debates about which hierarches are morally defensible and conducive to aggregate social welfare. Simply observing that hierarchies are natural gets us nowhere in such discussions.

For instance, few today would argue that a feudal hierarchy is justifiable, though many thinkers at the time tried to defend it by appealing to natural differences between people as ordained by the Christian God. This is because classical liberal thinkers argued that both the moral equality of individuals, and the need to increase aggregate welfare by engaging in market exchanges, entitles them to equally enjoy the standard package of liberal civil and political rights. Those who argue against the stark inequality of contemporary economic hierarchies—most notably liberal egalitarians like Rawls, Nussbaum, and Dworkin—make similar arguments to justify a more equitable distribution of goods and resources. Now one might disagree with the moral arguments for a more equitable distribution of goods and resources, or at least argue that a more equitable distribution would not be conducive to the aggregate welfare of all. These are the arguments thinkers like Nozick and Friedman respectively levelled against the liberal egalitarians. But neither the liberal egalitarians nor their opponents claim that their preferred hierarchies are "natural" to defend their respective positions. Instead they appeal to moral and empirical points to justify this or that given hierarchy.

Peterson's Politics Applied

So what do we make of Peterson's position? I think the unarticulated and implicit reasoning seems to be that current status quos are justifiable along the moral and empirical lines

I just mentioned; though he offers little in the way of moral argument and empirical evidence (angry moralism doesn't count). As mentioned, his justification for these positions often takes the form of individualized psychological advice with a political undertone. His justifications seem to be consistent in realizing that life is "unfair," hierarchy will always exist, and we must simply deal with it. He also argues that we stop resenting those who get ahead through merit and take responsibility for improving our own lot. So on the one hand we have fatalism about the status quo, on the other moralism about merit and getting ahead in contemporary hierarchies through effort.

As psychological advice for a person in need, either comment might be valid. The criteria is what the individual needs to hear in order to make sense of their situation and improve it. But when generalized as part of a political theory these two pieces of advice border on being mutually contradictory.

Take his comment that life is "suffering" and "unfair." If this is true by nature then individuals are largely fated to wind up where we are regardless of our particular effort and character. The rain will fall on the just and the unjust alike, poor people will work hard and not get ahead, and rich people will be born into advantages they did nothing to earn. In such a context, moralizing to individuals by telling them it is their fault for where they wound up because they didn't merit anything more would seem strikingly tactless. On the other hand, if it is true that life is "suffering" and "unfair" because of human institutions, not just by nature, this brings us back to the aforementioned problem I highlighted about which hierarchies can be justified. If human institutions are responsible for "suffering" and "unfairness," then simply advising people to apolitically accept this and make the best of it seems strikingly reactionary. Instead one should be making a concerted effort to change things. Indeed, for all Peterson's invocations of being a "classical liberal" he seems curiously disinterested in liberalism's historic concern to rectify injustices resulting from the persistence of illegitimate human institutions and hierarchies.

Conclusion

Peterson is an adept psychologist who offers useful advice to individuals in need of life guidance. In such contexts, drawing on a plethora of different sources, and offering fatalistic advice one day and promoting strident self-effort the next, might be useful. But generalized into political doctrine it becomes a rather confusing mish mash of distinct belief systems that don't gel into a coherent whole.

My suspicion, as with his critical observations about the Left, is that many of Peterson's readers feel an affinity for the advice he offers and so don't look to question his political commitments that deeply. This is problematic because it leads to deep inconsistencies in doctrine that, if applied as stated, would lead to a rather unusual politics. One stressing liberal freedom and Christian moralism, communal traditionalism and hyper individualism, and one assumes many other good things conveniently wrapped together. Politics may be complicated. But that is no excuse for generalizing anecdote and individual self-help into a comprehensive guide on how to order society.

On Marxism, Post-Modernism, and "Cultural Marxism"

Matt McManus

Introduction

In the post-modern epoch, it is increasingly common in Anglo-American circles to conflate post-modernism and Marxism under the label "cultural Marxism." Many of the authors in this book have discussed this at some length. The most famous and articulate contemporary figure is, of course, Professor Jordan Peterson. In his online lectures and recent bestseller *Twelve Rules for Life,* Peterson argues that Marxism's collapsing intellectual and moral credibility in the post-Stalinist era led to a crisis within left-wing thought. It had become clear that Marxist communism was no longer a morally viable outlook for anyone with sensitivity to the horrific consequences of the gulag. So, according to Peterson, many left wing intellectuals simply gave Marxism a new coat of paint to try and rejuvenate its credibility. Post-modern authors simply broadened Marxist ideas about class oppression to encompass all forms of social interaction. These post-modern figures now claimed that oppression and power existed everywhere, even in the most innocuous behaviors and cultures. So the point of left wing activism now became not simply to overthrow and oppress class structure or rectify drastic economic inequalities. It became to overturn every aspect of culture through criticizing it as racist, sexist, homophobic and so on and replace it with a vaguely defined egalitarian society, which is the post-modern equivalent of a communist utopia. Given this new emphasis on culture, and a perceived link with Leftism past, Peterson has taken to calling post-modernists "cultural Marxists."

Peterson is joined in this appraisal by a litany of other, less sophisticated commentators. Ben Shapiro has consistently called on conservatives and classical liberals to combat the growing influence of cultural Marxism. Matthew Continetti of the *National Review* wrote a column on "the coalition for cultural freedom" and praised Peterson (amongst others) for combatting a resurgent Marxism on university campuses. In my own country of Canada, the *National Post's* Barbara Kay ridiculed that "Marxism marinated cultural elites obsessed with group rather than individual rights." And the litany against cultural Marxism goes on.

There is a highly reactionary quality to much of this discourse, not to mention a rather homogenizing effort to conflate all variants of far left discourse under one convenient label. Frankly, at points it feels that the Cold War never really ended for some of these authors. This has resulted in a consistent lack of rigor and analytical clarity when assessing the state of today's left wing movements. Here, I want to dedicate some time to indicating why Marxism and post-modernism are intellectually quite different. Indeed, in many respects the latter is quite fundamentally different at both a theoretical and a practical level. Understanding why this is so will help us gain a better understanding of what makes today's radical left different (and what makes it the same).

What is Marxism?

Marxism emerged in the 19th century from a novel (if often shaky) fusion of Hegelian historicism, French political radicalism, and English political economy. This synthesis of influences reflected Marx's biographical trajectory. As a young scholar at the University of Bonn, and later the University of Berlin, Marx initially studied law but quickly became enamored with philosophy. He wrote his Doctoral dissertation, *The Difference Between Democritean and Epicurean Philosophies of Nature,* defending a more materialist and scientific approach to nature against what he took to be the superstitions of theology. Later, Marx became enamored with the thought of Georg Hegel and the Young Hegelians, collaborating with his friend and supporter Friedrich Engels to turn Hegel right side up and make his idealist dialectical philosophy more materialist. After parlaying with the French socialists and Anarchists, he was exiled from several countries before landing in the United Kingdom. He published the first volume of his masterwork, *Das Kapital*, in 1867, but was never able to complete the others in his lifetime. He died a relatively well-off middle class gentleman in London in 1883 after spending most of his last decade reading Shakespeare and writing (apparently bad) poetry.

Were he alive today, Marx would likely have responded to the claim that he was a post-modern theorist with sarcastic ridicule. Brought up in an Enlightenment friendly household, he was deeply concerned to present his work as a scientific and materially grounded analysis of capitalist society. Whatever one thinks of that pretension, he would no doubt find the association with so called "relativists," "identity politics," and the destruction of the West's literary and cultural heritage cloying.

Marxism is a complex doctrine that cannot possibly be summarized here. I will limit myself to a few observations about its main tenets. Firstly, Marx's analysis of capitalist society was predicated on his philosophical and methodological commitment to historical materialism. Summarized very briefly, Marx accepted the then popular scientific view that in one sense the world consists of atomically separated objects. However, he broke with dogmatic empiricism in arguing that what is more important than the independence of these objects is the relations that existed between them. Take for instance a tree. While it is a material object in the world, seen in isolation, it is a fairly dead incidental thing that is abstractly understood. To try to understand a tree, one must grasp the "dialectical" relations it has with the world around it; taking in solar energy from the sun, nutrients and water, releasing oxygen into the air and so forth.

This was integral to his understanding of society. His criticism of the classical "vulgar economists" of his day were drawn from this dialectical philosophy. He saw classical economists as essentially regarding individuals as abstractly isolated in the world. From their standpoint, individuals looked after their private needs by engaging in mutually beneficial bartering and exchanges with others that were non-coercive and so legitimate. As per the tree example, Marx saw this as a very abstract way of looking at the economy. It was divorced from the actual relations that existed between people which had emerged from a complex and often violent history. One example is private property. According to Marx, classical political economists were ahistorical in looking at the economy as just a process of buying and selling between individuals. It was also defined by relations between those who had started with a great deal, again often acquired through violent primitive accumulation, and those with far less. Those with a great deal, the bourgeois capitalists, were typically able to dictate the terms by which those with less, the proletariat, were able to participate in the economy. For instance, because they owned the means of production where most people could find employment, the capitalists were largely able to determine the wages they were going to pay people, even if that was not consonant with the work they committed and the value they created. This is what led to exploitation. This exploitation was hidden from most people by what Marx termed ideology; the abstract set of norms and rules that hid the real truth of complex material processes of appropriation and exploitation from the mass of society.

This is an interesting story. Whether it is true or not is not at issue here. What I want to observe is that ontologically and epistemically Marx is 1) highly committed to a theory of truth:

dialectical materialism, and 2) believed that this truth could be uncovered by getting past "ideology." Conjoined to this ontological and epistemic stance is a strong moral commitment to ridding society of perceived exploitation—though Marx was hesitant to ever directly invoke the language of morality. As we shall see, this is quite different from the position of one school of post-modern theorists.

What is Post-Modernism?

I like to divide left wing post-modern theorists into two schools of thought. The first school of thought is composed of scholars who understand post-modernism as an epoch in Western history. Most are self-identified Marxists or post-Marxists. Representative thinkers include Frederic Jameson, David Harvey, Jean Francois Lyotard, Neil Postman and Jean Baudrillard. Ironically these authors often agree with many conservative criticisms of the post-modern epoch. They argue that social, economic, and technological changes have brought about a society where individuals increasingly look solely to their own private opinions, and those that agree with them, for epistemic and moral authority. They reject truth claims from other groups, seeing those as antithetical to their interests. To provide a brief (and telling) example, Neil Postman and Jean Baudrillard both wrote about how the hyper-real modern media, with its heightened rhetoric and two minute analysis, was having a dramatic impact on how people understand political and moral positions. By increasingly reducing the dissemination of information to clearly partisan and simplified sound bites, the media was creating a world where people felt that all truth claims were nothing but opinion. They, like the other authors in this school, were highly critical of this development because they accorded truth a great deal of significance.

The second school of left wing post-modernism is slightly different, taking a stronger critical stance on truth. This school largely emerged in the aftermath of the May 1968 protests and riots, and reacted very strongly against Marxism and its aspirations for scientific truth and world-historical applicability. While authors in this school were open to the possibility that new and better theories of truth might be developed, they were skeptical that we would ever arrive at a theory that gave us both uninhibited access to the world, and moral certainty. They were, to invoke Richard Rorty, anti-Archimedeans. There was likely no standpoint from which to get at the truth. Unlike authors in the first school, they did not regard these epistemic and moral conclusions as contingent on epochal social circumstances. They regarded them as valid for all time. Conjoined to this epistemic and moral skepticism was an analysis of power dynamics which were responsible for making flimsy or problematic truth claims seem valid. Canonical (pun intended) authors in this line of thinking include Michel Foucault, Jacques Derrida, Bruno Latour, and America's own Richard Rorty.

Conclusion

Personally, I tend to think there is a great deal one can learn from the first school of post-modern authors, and less from the second. Indeed, many conservative critics such as Patrick Deneen and Allan Bloom might well sympathize with claims that our media-saturated hyper-real environment is dissolving our capacity to assess truth claims. But that is not the issue here.

Most authors in the first school are highly critical of post-modern culture. They actually hold to the old Marxist line that one can obtain "true" epistemic insight into the nature of society. While they don't necessarily share Marx's hyper-scientific pretentions, they feel that the point of theory is to get past "ideology" in order to arrive at universalizable conclusions about what is and what should be done. The authors in the second school of post-modern thought don't share this conclusion. Reacting very strongly against Marx and Marxism, they reject the idea of "ideology" because they do not believe there is any way to get past discursive power to arrive at what really is and what should be done. They also are deeply skeptical of claims that one can establish a non-exploitative society. They regard strong moral arguments like this as a potential mask for establishing new forms of marginalization and dismissal. To the extent that they moralize at all, contra Marx, authors in the second school tend to appeal to highly individualist Nietzschian arguments about self-creation and aesthetic rapture as a (very vague) new moral outlook. Many of the identity politics acolytes who draw on post-modern theory share this outlook. Very little in this is consonant with any recognizable Marxist doctrine.

What this brief genealogy shows us is that the attempt to conflate Marxism and post-modernism under the label "cultural Marxism" is, at the very least, highly problematic. Theorists who wrote about post-modernism as an epoch drew on Marx and post-Marxist ideas to criticize it very sharply. Those who wrote about post-modernism as a philosophical stance, and who are the main theoretical inspirations for today's identity politics advocates tended to be highly critical, or in Foucault's case even dismissive, of Marx. Critics on the right who want to lump all strands of left wing intellectual thought together should be far more cautious and rigorous in their appraisals. Otherwise they're just knocking down caricatures and strawmen.

Hillary's America, Bowling for Columbine, and Post-Modern Conservative Cinema Aesthetics

David Hollands

Robin Wood, *Triumph of the Will,* and *Night and Fog*

In the second chapter of *Sexual Politics and Narrative Film: Hollywood and Beyond,* published in 1998, the late critic Robin Wood places two documentaries in dialogue: the infamous Leni Riefenstahl-directed Nazi propaganda piece *Triumph of the Will* (1935) and Alain Resnais' poetic *Night and Fog* (1956)—the former a celebration of Nazi ideology and the latter a haunting exploration of who ultimately bears responsibility for the unimaginable atrocities committed during the Holocaust. Wood compares and contrasts the two films in order to demonstrate that the kinds of art they represent to audiences, critics, and film theorists are impossible to separate from their ideological significance. While this may seem like an obvious point to make in 1998, let alone in this current context, Wood is, in fact, responding to critics—John Russell Taylor in particular—who were still holding the position that *Triumph of the Will* is able to transcend—to use Wood's word—its own content and to be viewed purely as a film in and of itself. Wood refers to this reclaiming of *Triumph of the Will* as a beautiful piece of art divorced from its screamingly obvious politics as the typical "liberal" view of the film, a view that Wood resists adamantly. For Wood, the aesthetics of *Triumph of the Will*—the low-angled tracking shots of Hitler travelling through Germany to adoring crowds, the frightening scope of the Nuremberg rallies, Hitler's speeches, again filmed at oppressive low angles—are Nazi/ fascist aesthetics, period, full stop. Their primary purpose is to force its audience to submit to its ideology. Wood believes that any attempt to divorce that ideological meaning from the film's stylistics is ignoring the reality that what we as audiences find aesthetically striking is primarily culturally determined.

By contrast, Wood's interpretation of *Night and Fog* is more ambiguous. Wood views *Night and Fog* as a film that attempts to inspire contemplation in audiences rather than psychological submission. The film's primary means of compelling contemplation in its audience is through its aesthetics. Resnais uses a number of stylistic devices—musical counterpoint, emotionally detached voice-over narration—to attempt to inspire his audience to engage with the filmic text analytically. In Wood's own words,

"[the] achieved [stylistic] distance has the effect, paradoxically, of *increasing* awareness of the appalling nature of what we are shown: instead of being numbed by horrors, the spectator's capacity for thought, imagination, and empathy is given scope and freedom. [...] The entire film is built on a complex pattern of formal alternations that foreground the medium, so that the sense of actuality is constantly paralleled by an awareness of filmic discourse: present/past, color/black-and-white, moving film/stills, stylized camera movement/authentic newsreel. We are encouraged—up to a certain point—to *think* about what we see."

Despite Resnais' efforts, Wood feels the film falls short in a standard "liberal" fashion at its conclusion, where concentration camp authorities on trial refuse responsibility for the mass murders of the Holocaust. For Wood, the film leaves audiences with the question, "*Who* is responsible?" rather than, "*What* is responsible?" While Wood finds the stylistic distance of the film admirable, he also clearly feels that that distance is ultimately one of the film's overall shortcomings; in refusing to point directly at the authorities' ideological adherence to Nazism as a root cause of the atrocities that occurred, *Night and Fog* is leaving audiences with a specific kind of "liberal" despair, one that does not encourage inspiration to bring about positive change to the world. Wood's own words on the matter are pointed:

"What the ending leaves us with is liberalism's familiar hands-in-the-air gesture of appalled helplessness: these things have happened before; they will happen (and today are happening) again; they are a part of nature or 'the human condition'; there is nothing we can do except try to remember, and memory always fails."

Even more pointed is Wood's assertion that with the creations of the institutions of private property and patriarchy, out of which marriage, monogamy, and the patriarchal family emerge, come the seeds and tendencies of the fascist society:

"The fascist society, then, which *Triumph of the Will* gives us a privileged opportunity to examine in detail, simply carries to their logical conclusion many of the tendencies present in the society in which we live and by which we cannot fail to be contaminated."

Wood identifies some of these fascist tendencies as an emphasis on the procreative role of the family to perpetuate the dominant race through the rigid definition of gender roles, including the subordination of women within the family, a sense of strict sexual morality, and a persecution of non-heteronormative sexualities. These tendencies that Wood identifies that I have just mentioned are obviously still hotly contested, and it is not the purpose of this essay to reiterate these ongoing ideological debates and clashes, to agree with Wood's claims wholeheartedly, or to dismiss them;that statement probably identifies me as the kind of "liberal" Wood would have been suspicious of, to put it charitably. I have summarized Wood here to provide an understanding of what he means by fascism, which is important in comprehending both his revulsion of *Triumph of the Will* and his critique of *Night and Fog*. Also, having a sense of Wood's understanding of fascism helps us in comprehending his following claim that popular or dominant cinema contains fascistic elements. Wood believes strongly that the oppressive elements of our current society that I have outlined above are embedded in every aspect of cinema, including the specific kinds of camera movements and editing—what Wood calls camera rhetoric—used by Riefenstahl in *Triumph of the Will*; for Wood, the aesthetics of *Triumph of the Will* are by no means exclusive to that film, and are often employed as "common [cinematic] currency" in American and European cinema, popular or otherwise. His position therefore echoes Benjamin's as presented in "The Work of Art in the Age of Mechanical Reproduction," which is explored in greater depth in this anthology.

Cinema and Post-Modern Conservatism: Beginning the Discussion

Earlier in this anthology, Matthew McManus identifies post-modern conservatism as an exacerbated continuation of the irrationalism of Edmund Burke. According to McManus, post-modern conservatism "disdains belief in objective truth and mores [...] and locates meaning in a reactionary identity and its values" in ways that are designed to allow post-modern conservatives to remain "faithful to a conservative identity" by almost any means necessary. Much like what Robin Wood attempts in his second chapter of *Sexual Politics and Narrative Film: Hollywood and Beyond*, I wish to begin a conversation on how post-modern conservatism manifests aesthetically in cinema. A full study of this question is well beyond the scope of this essay, though I will take a few initial steps by offering a brief analysis of two documentaries: *Hillary's America: The Secret History of the Democratic Party* (2016) (hereafter *Hillary's America*), by the controversial conservative author and filmmaker Dinesh D'Souza, and *Bowling for Columbine* (2002), the infamous exploration of American gun culture by left-wing muckraker Michael Moore. Both films are documentaries, and both are examples of what Bill Nichols calls the expository and participatory modes. Both forcefully communicate ideological messages on opposite sides of the political spectrum, and, surprisingly, both are similar—though not equal, certainly—in terms of their aesthetic strategies.

Hillary's America presents its own particular history of the Democratic Party of the United States. According to the film, the Democrat-Republican switch—where regressive and overtly racist democrats eventually switched party allegiances for a variety of complex reasons over a period that lasted roughly from the 1860s to the mid-1930s—is a liberal myth. The "truth," as presented in *Hillary's America,* is that the Democratic Party is now covertly racist, and uses social welfare programs targeted at low-income urban areas to coerce its largely minority and lower-class voter base into perpetual servitude to the party.

How do the aesthetics of *Hillary's America* potentially make this overly simplistic and conspiratorial account of the Democratic Party palpable to a post-modern conservative audience? The documentary is primarily structured as a series of interviews interspersed with dramatized recreations of the interviewees' claims—and, by extension, the arguments D'Souza wills his audience to accept. The recreations themselves make use of a number of obvious cinematic tricks—low angles, chiaroscuro lighting, discordant music on the soundtrack, slow tracking shots or push-ins—to attempt to inspire alarmism and fear in the audience whenever the film means to emphasize the inherent evil of the Democratic Party. The film also foregrounds a fascistic kind of nationalism by portraying an idealized version of America that the Democratic Party wishes to destroy. This ideal manifests in the film as a kind of hyperactive version of the country as the "land of opportunity" where the same fascistic impulses that the documentary revels in have apparently been snuffed. What is most remarkable about *Hillary's America* is that this idealized America is portrayed almost entirely through symbolism. One of the climactic moments of the film, a montage of an orchestra playing "The Star-Spangled Banner," almost seems like it could be a modern remake of *Triumph of the Will*, at least aesthetically speaking. The four-minute sequence begins with D'Souza imploring his audience to vote for Donald Trump in the 2016 election, and transitions to the aforementioned orchestral rendition of the national anthem. Shots of the orchestra playing are intercut with amusingly kitschy images such as Civil War-era canons being fired, a soldier standing in a wheat field at dusk waving Old Glory in slow motion, more soldiers raising the American flag at Iwo Jima, an image of fighter jets doing a flyover *reflected in the orchestra's organ pipes*, a man parasailing with a giant American flag blowing behind him, again in slow motion, and fireworks igniting near the Statue of Liberty at night, to name a few. The sequence is designed to have a maximum affective impact on D'Souza's audience, much in the same way that similar passages in *Triumph of the Will* were meant to be impactful for German audiences in 1935. This kind of hyper-affective sensationalism is a prominent feature of D'Souza's film. Given that this sensationalism is also prominent in the theatrical trailer for D'Souza's next effort, *Death of a Nation* (2018), as well as his documentaries prior to *Hillary's America*, I feel that I am on the correct track in proposing that the aesthetics of post-modern conservative cinema will continue to be mobilized by conservative filmmakers in the ways described above. More work needs to be done to identify potential historical precursors to this hyper-affective form of post-modern conservative aesthetics, and, of course, to test if this claim holds up across a number of different examples.

I began this essay with an exposition of Robin Wood's contrasting of *Triumph of the Will* with *Night and Fog*. While it may seem that I am about to claim that *Night and Fog* is more in line with *Bowling for Columbine*, since I compared the aesthetics of *Triumph of the Will* with those of *Hillary's America*, my point in bringing *Hillary's America* and *Bowling for Columbine* into dialogue with each other is to demonstrate that, like Wood's claims about fascistic tendencies embedded in the discourse of American and European cinema, elements of what has possibly become post-modern conservative cinema aesthetics were already present in works that were not politically and ideologically conservative.

Michael Moore is a sensationalist filmmaker who is prone to aesthetic hyperbole and factual manipulation, though not nearly to the same degree as Dinesh D'Souza is in his own work. In fact, *Bowling for Columbine* presents an inversion of how Wood described the conclusion of *Night and Fog*: the film explicitly identifies what it presents as the political and ideological problems of American culture and its relation to gun violence, yet it does so in ways that do not necessarily allow for analytical distance. While the emotional appeals of *Bowling for Columbine* are not nearly as hyper-affective as those of *Hillary's America*, they are still present to a lesser degree and are used to convince the audience of Moore's arguments via pathos. One montage in particular, set to Louis Armstrong's "What a Wonderful World," where Moore summarizes a chronicle of events from 1953, when the U.S. overthrew Prime Minister Mossadeq of Iran, to the terrorist attacks of September 11th, 2001, is meant to present an inarguable history of recent U.S. foreign policy, and support Moore's thesis that there is little difference between the Columbine High School shootings and America's direct influence on the world stage. Whether Moore is correct or not is not the issue; rather, how this segment is presented stylistically is crucial to examine. While haunting, the montage is undoubtedly manipulative, though in a subtler way than the montage described above from *Hillary's America.* It is the song that is the primary manipulative force in this sequence; the song is an obvious counterpoint to the images presented, and makes Moore's arguments abundantly clear.

There are other, by-now infamous examples of manipulation

through editing in *Bowling for Columbine*. One such example is how the film frames Charlton Heston's NRA speeches. Facts are manipulated via subtle editing in order for Moore to launch an attack on Heston, who becomes an avatar of sorts for America's gun violence problems. Specifically, footage of Heston delivering his speech at an NRA convention in Littleton, the town where the Columbine High School shooting took place, is manipulated to make the speech appear to be morally tasteless. Moore, in fact, pulled some lines from a different speech in Littleton given a year prior, such as Heston's proud declaration, "From my cold, dead hands!" This is evident in the film when, shortly after Heston begins his main speech, his outfit changes completely, indicating that two different recordings have been spliced together. There is often no overtly obvious indication of manipulation in *Bowling for Columbine* as there is in *Hillary's America*. The strange paradox of post-modern conservative cinema aesthetics is that while its hyper-affective sensibilities are incredibly seductive for certain audiences, these sensibilities are also much easier to identify and critique. The subtler manipulations that Moore uses require more perceptive eyes. *Bowling for Columbine* can potentially be seen as a film that uses earlier forms of what would predict post-modern conservative cinema aesthetics.

Conclusion

I do not agree entirely with Robin Wood's claim that elements of fascist aesthetics are necessarily embedded and reflected in American and European cinema discourse in general. There are other obvious traditions that Wood seems to displace or ignore in *Sexual Politics and Narrative Film: Hollywood and Beyond*, such as the influence of Eisenstein's dialectical montage on filmmakers as wide-ranging as Fritz Lang to Alfred Hitchcock. Eisenstein, of course, emerged as a significant filmmaker and film theorist in the Soviet Union during the 1920s, which would suggest that fascist sensibilities are one of many potential aesthetic wells upon which cinema draws.

That being stated, there are clear examples of fascistic cinema discourses that one can point to in a number of different historical contexts. I have attempted to use both *Hillary's America* and *Bowling for Columbine* to show one overt example of how post-modern conservative cinema aesthetics is comparable to fascist cinema discourse, and to demonstrate that the seeds for such an aesthetic turn in cinema were already at least planted in an earlier work of opposing political ideology. If it turns out that post-modern conservative cinema aesthetics continue to be identifiable in a significantly larger number of films, either already released or soon-to-be, then another progeny of the fascist aesthetic impulse has been identified.

No Future? Think Again!: The Peterson Phenomenon, Capitalist Realism, and the Idea of Communism

Borna Radnik

Introduction

It feels strange to write about postmodernism in the 21st century. I use the term "strange" because postmodernism, with its emphasis on fragmentation, difference, self-referentiality, irony and pastiche, is a relic of the past. Or at least it feels as though it is a relic of the past; a hangover from the 1980s and 90s. One of the distinctive features of the postmodern is that it rejects the "grand narratives" of modernism. Grand narratives such as the concept of universal truth, or the idea that history advances and progresses through some form of teleology are both things which postmodernism is hostile to. Postmodernity resists any and all attempts to systematically champion any form of universal narration, and instead privileges the fragmentary, the individuated, and the distinctive aspects of cultural phenomena and human experience. If these descriptions of the postmodern seem abstract and vague that is because postmodernism itself, as a concept, is notoriously difficult to accurately define and pin down. In popular culture, the word "postmodernism" conjures up images of fragmented narration in films like Quentin Tarantino's *Pulp Fiction*; and self-referential films such as Charlie Kaufman's *Adaptation* (where the protagonist—Charlie Kaufman—is hired to write an adapted screenplay of *The Orchid Thief* and ends up writing himself into the screenplay). In the world of fiction, we may think of Thomas Pynchon's arduous *Gravity's Rainbow* which is "often considered as the postmodern novel."

Yet for all its pervasiveness in popular culture, the definition of postmodernism remains ambiguous. In philosophy, for example, postmodernism has been used as an umbrella term to describe a constellation of French thinkers that came into prominence after the Second World War. Figures such as Michel Foucault, Jacques Derrida, Jean-François Lyotard, and Gilles Deleuze are just some of the philosophers that have been described as postmodern. While it is true that these theorists are, all in their own unique way, critical of modernity, it must be noted, however, that ironically enough they never referred to themselves as postmodern thinkers. The application of the term "postmodern" to describe French philosophy of the 1960s to 1990s is largely an Anglo-American retroactive invention. If the label of postmodernism ostensibly designates a catch-all constellation of multiple thinkers, then, to borrow a phrase from Jack Gilbert: "we must unlearn the constellation to see the stars." It does a serious disservice to these disparate philosophers if we reduce them all to a single, homogenous label. However, writing about postmodernism in our century is strange for another reason, namely that the heyday of the postmodern as a topic of theoretical debate and discussion is long over, spanning roughly twenty years, from 1979 to 1999. As the second decade of the 21st century draws to a close, we may find ourselves agreeing with Peter Osborne's recent diagnosis that (within the world of art theory) "the category of postmodernism is now well and truly buried."

If the concept of postmodernity is actually truly buried in intellectual circles, one would think that we would let the dead bury the dead and move on. Yet, postmodernism, it seems, has been brought back from the dead. Postmodernism is enjoying somewhat of a second life in the popular discourse. Its zombie-like resurrection is perhaps best exemplified in the work of Canadian clinical psychologist and University of Toronto Professor, Jordan B. Peterson. In the past couple of years, Peterson has managed to garner a cult following of thousands, mostly through his popular online YouTube lectures. The once obscure academic began his online fame in 2016 by posting a YouTube video in which he voices his criticism for Canada's Bill-C 16, a bill sought to amend the Canadian Human Rights Act by including and extending legal protections to gender identity and gender expression. Peterson, however, fears that the amendments to include gender identity and expression in the Human Rights Act amounts to nothing more than an attack on the individual civil liberty of free speech because, at least according to Peterson, the amendments compel individuals by force of law to use gender preferred pronouns to refer to non-binary people. As Peterson declared in a televised discussion "if they fine me, I won't pay it. If they put me in jail, I'll go on a hunger strike. I'm not doing this. And that's that. I'm not using the words that other people require me to use. Especially if they're made up by radical left-wing ideologues." Despite the fact that Peterson is empirically wrong about the practical ramifications of the recent amendments (Brenda Cossman has pointed out that Peterson's alarmist declarations have no legal traction), his outspoken refusal to accept "compelled speech" by "radical left-wing ideologues" has nevertheless contributed to his online fame. It is this popularity, and its social and political context, that interests me in this chapter.

Not only is Peterson demonstrably wrong about the practical effects of Canada's now-passed Bill C-16, he is also wrong about the supposed threat of "radical left-wing ideologues," which he thinks coincide with postmodernism. In Peterson's lectures, postmodernism functions as the discursive bogeyman of all things that are wrong with the "extreme Left." In his YouTube lectures, and his recent bestseller *12 Rules for Life: An Antidote to Chaos*, Peterson admonishes the cultural and societal ills of our times, and partly blames what he (falsely) believes to be the rise of "post-modern, Cultural Marxists." As many critics of Peterson have already pointed out, Marxism and "postmodernism" are not only different traditions (if we can even refer to postmodernism as a tradition), but are explicitly incompatible with one another. Marxism amounts to just another universal grand narrative, something which postmodern theory would not accept without discursive qualifications and reservations. Given that the academic debates about postmodernism are nearly twenty years old, it is curious that Peterson perceives it as an ongoing political threat emanating from university campuses. While Peterson undoubtedly (and perhaps deliberately) misuses the term "postmodernism" to deride and denounce what he claims to be the concerted work of "radical left-wing ideologues" to undermine (neo)liberal cultural norms and mores, his international fame is indicative of a much larger cultural shift that has been taking place since the 2008 financial crisis.

The Peterson phenomenon is deeply symptomatic of a broader, structural shift in the global capitalist order. As Slavoj Žižek, Nathan J. Robinson, and others have pointed out, Peterson's popularity can be partly attributed to the social and cultural vacuum he seems to fill for thousands who are disappointed and frustrated with the lack of direction in their lives and feel hopeless about the future. Peterson's rise to fame is indicative of an all-too pervasive socio-economic trend that has been amplified since the 2008 financial crisis. Walter Benjamin theorized that every rise of fascism emerges from the failure of a radical revolution. Peterson's fame coincides with the emergence of white supremacy and nationalism in North America and Europe. Both the Peterson phenomenon and the resurgence of nationalism are reactions to the economic instability that ruptured in the 2008 crisis, an instability that is inherent to the capitalist mode of production. This predicament has been remarked upon by Žižek, who comments on the 2016 U.S. elections: "The popular rage which gave birth to Trump also gave birth to Sanders, and while they both express widespread social and political discontent, they do it in opposite senses, the one engaging in Rightist populism and the other opting for the

Leftist call for justice." Similarly, Franco "Bifo" Berardi asserts that:

> "Brexit and Trump's electoral victory marked a breakpoint in the history of neoliberal globalism. In the past century, we thought democracy and socialism had defeated nationalism. Wrong. Nationalism is back, thanks to the vengeance of the white working class, humiliated by neoliberal policies and betrayed by social reformists who have played into the hands of the financial dictatorship. "

Not only is populist nationalism back in fashion, but it is becoming increasingly more difficult to theorize our historical present. The 2008 financial crisis reinforced, within the cultural sphere, the lack of what Frederic Jameson calls a cognitive map. According to Jameson, a cognitive map is a clear, subjective understanding of one's place in a global political or cultural system. Jameson's concept of the cognitive map is our cultural collective imaginary, our political coordinates with which we comprehend our present. This lack of a cognitive map in our present historical moment is symptomatic of the capitalist political economy. The late Mark Fisher builds on Jameson's work, and refers to this cultural confusion, or lack of political imagination, as *capitalist realism*. For Fisher, capitalist realism is "the widespread sense that not only is capitalism the only viable political and economic system, but also that it is now impossible even to *imagine* a coherent alternative to it."

In the 21st century, it is becoming abundantly clear that there is no alternative to capitalism. What was once an alternative, communism, needs to be seriously rethought in its actualization. Jordan Peterson, and his demagogic use of cultural buzzwords such as "postmodernism," despite the decline of academic interest in the topic, is best understood in terms of Fisher's notion of capitalist realism. The fame Peterson enjoys is a symptom of capital realism. His fans and followers primarily consist of white men who feel alienated and frustrated by the dominant liberal ideological discourse of identity politics. This hopelessness about a future is a symptom of capitalist realism. Peterson's inflammatory rhetoric against the discourse of identity politics emboldens far-Right reactionaries and white supremacists. I argue that in order to properly appreciate and understand the Peterson Phenomenon we have to situate Peterson's notoriety within the context of capitalist realism. There are three dialectically intertwined registers that contribute to our understanding of the Peterson phenomenon: 1) cultural register; 2) political register; and 3) the revolutionary register. There is a dialectical relationship between the popularity of far-Right, white nationalists, figures such as Peterson, and finance capital's contraction and expansion. Before we can appreciate how Fisher's concept of capitalist realism applies to the case of Peterson's fame and the political context of Peterson's following, we first need to see how Fisher goes beyond Jameson's original diagnosis of the culture of capitalism.

Cultural Register: Capitalist Realism

The concept of the postmodern is not something that can be easily defined. If we follow Jameson, then, postmodernism names the culturally dominant expression of "late" capitalism. To this extent, postmodernism is effectively a periodization of the capitalist political economy. However, as Peter Osborne rightly indicated, intellectual interest in postmodernity seems to be a thing of the past, nearly twenty years old to be exact (1979-1999). As the force of postmodernism waned, the early-2000s saw a renewed theoretical interest in modernism. As Osborne puts it, there has been "a revival, deepening, multiplication and complication of discourses of the modern – with 'multiple,' 'alternative,' and 'postcolonial' modernities at the fore – accompanied and followed by the decline of the category of the postmodern from the mid-1990s onwards." Even Jameson himself devotes an entire book to the rebirth of interest in the various themes of modernist philosophy and theory. Osborne is quick to note, however, that these revived modernist discourses have not been able to sufficiently comprehend "the most distinctive cultural features (that is, the lived novelty) of the/our historical present." One possible explanation for why neither the concept of postmodernity, nor the renewed discourses of "alternate modernities" adequately capture the cultural logic of 21st century capitalism is due to our collective deficiency in what Jameson calls a cognitive map. For Jameson, a cognitive map refers to "a pedagogical political culture which seeks to endow the individual subject with some new heightened sense of its place in the global system." We no longer enjoy such an instructive political culture, and it is this lack of political cognitive mapping that is best articulated by Fisher's concept of capitalist realism. It is precisely under the cultural aegis of capitalist realism that Jordan Peterson is able to thrive and profit.

What is becoming increasingly clear at the turn of our century is that our collective cultural utopian imaginary is stagnant, if not altogether utterly impotent. As Jameson admits, it is now much easier to imagine the end of the world than to imagine the end of capitalism as a political and social system. Mark Fisher extends this cultural impotence through his concept of capitalist realism. As a cultural malaise, capitalist realism—the general sense that there is no alternative to capitalism—seems to reign absolute. While the concept of capitalist realism emerges from postmodernity, Fisher argues that there are three features that distinguish the former from the latter. First, that with the theoretical debate around postmodernism that peaked in the 1980s there was still "in name at least, political alternatives to capitalism." Second, postmodernism was decidedly a reaction against all things modern, and in this sense bore some relation to modernity. Capitalist realism has no such relationship with modernism. Third, an entire generation (or more) has passed since the end of the Cold War and the fall of the Berlin Wall; millennials have grown up with no existing alternative (not even in name only) to capitalism. One of the consequences of this last feature of capitalist realism is that "capitalism seamlessly occupies the horizons of the thinkable." Indeed, in the 21st century there "is a deeper, far more pervasive, sense of exhaustion, of cultural and political sterility."

What the 2008 financial crisis effectively demonstrated, was that capital does not necessarily require liberal democracy to thrive. As an ideology, neoliberalism failed to adequately manage the aftershocks of the 2008 financial crisis. Both Brexit in the UK, and Trump's electoral victory in the U.S. are two exemplary dominant symptoms of an ideological shift to the far-Right on a global scale. The Overton window has moved away from the "safe" confines of neoliberalism and has been shifting to the Right. The 2008 crisis signaled the end of neoliberalism as the dominant ideology of capitalism. Fisher rightly notes that:

"Despite initial appearances (and hopes), capitalist realism was not undermined by the credit crisis of 2008. The speculation, that capitalism might be on the verge of collapsing soon proved to be unfounded. It quickly became clear that, far from constituting the end of capitalism, the bank bail-outs were a massive re-assertion of the capitalist realist insistence that there is no alternative. [...] What did happen in 2008 was the collapse of the framework which has provided ideological cover for capitalist accumulation since the 1970s. [...] We can now see that, while neoliberalism was necessarily capitalist realist, capitalist realism need not be neoliberal. In order to save itself, capitalism could revert to a model of social democracy or to a *Children of Men*-like authoritarianism. Without a credible and coherent alternative to capitalism, capitalist realism will continue to rule the political economic unconscious."

Therefore, if it is indeed Jameson's original analysis that

postmodernism is the cultural expression of capital in its transition from the welfare model to the neoliberal model, and if neoliberalism's reign as the New World Order is over, then it is not a coincidence that postmodernism as a topic of intellectual discussion has seriously declined after the turn of the century. While it is a relic of the 1990s in academic circles, there are certain traces and vestiges of postmodernism—such as irony, subversion, and transgression— that still permeate throughout our culture. Furthermore, the erasure of the neoliberal order correlates to the solidification of capitalist realism. What we are witnessing now (Trumpism, the emboldening of the far-right nationalism in Europe and North America, and so on), is a symptom of capital ideologically transitioning into something altogether new and dangerous: no longer merely neoliberal, but far-Right, reactionary, and politically authoritarian form of capitalism. In this respect, Fisher's use of the 2006 film *Children of Men* is perhaps more appropriate for our times than he could have ever imagined.

Political Register: Did Somebody Say "Fascism"?

With the slow decay of the neoliberal ideology, it has become somewhat of a sport in our turbulent times to compare Trump's ascent in the U.S. to the rise of Hitler in 1930s Germany. The best representative of the impulse to compare Hitler and Trump is perhaps Timothy Snyder, who in his book *On Tyranny: Twenty Lessons from the Twentieth Century,* boldly asserts that

> "In the late nineteenth century, just as in the late twentieth century, the expansion of global trade generated expectations of progress. In the early twentieth century, as in the early twenty-first, these hopes were challenged by new visions of mass politics in which a leader or a party claimed to directly represent the will of the people. European democracies collapsed into right-wing authoritarianism and fascism in

> the 1920s and '30s. The communist Soviet Union, established in 1922, extended its model into Europe in the 1940s. The European history of the twentieth century shows us that societies can break, democracies can fall, ethics can collapse, and ordinary men can find themselves standing over death pits with guns in their hands. It would serve us well today to understand why."

This attempt to draw parallels to the emergence of totalitarian movements is common on both the left and the right. Most notably, Jordan Peterson has garnered significant attention by deploying the term "cultural Marxism" to denigrate left wing radicals. The term "cultural Marxism," is a common phrase in the conspiratorial discourse of the far-Right in America. Tanner Mirrlees notes that while "Peterson is not a fascist and he often says he hates Nazis," Peterson's "deployment of 'cultural Marxism' as a term of opprobrium when ranting against 'political correctness' and 'social justice' in Canada appeals to reactionaries worldwide." While Peterson himself may not be a fascist, it is nevertheless crucial to bear in mind that the term "cultural Marxism" is not unlike the propaganda term "cultural Bolshevism" (*Kulturbolschewismus*) used by the Nazi Party to denounce and discredit various artists and intellectuals such as Charlie Chaplin and Albert Einstein in the 1920s and 1930s. Indeed, it is worth remembering that under the leadership of Joseph Goebbels, the Nazis founded the Public Enlightenment and Propaganda Ministry in 1933. Richard J. Evans reminds us that "the most immediate aim of Nazi cultural politics was to dispose of the 'cultural Bolshevism' which various organs and representatives of the Nazi Party had declared was infesting the artistic, musical, and literary world of the Weimar Republic." Mirrlees notes how "in post-Cold War America, paleo-conservative think-tanks and white nationalist organizations" rebranded the term "cultural Bolshevikism" as "cultural

Marxism." Peterson uses "cultural Marxism" as a pejorative against what he thinks are far-Left, postmodernists that are dangerous and corrosive to society. One wonders whether or not Peterson is aware of the political history of the rhetoric he so liberally employs.

Whatever his motivations, Peterson's scorn for cultural Marxism has made him a celebrity to the alt-right, who in the words of Angela Nagle are "a new wave of overtly white segregationist and white nationalist movements and subcultures, typified by spokespeople like Richard Spencer, who has called for a US white ethnostate and a pan-national white empire." While the continuing rise of Right-wing nationalism and white supremacists in the U.S., and U.K., and other European countries is definitely alarming, one of the features that differentiates the alt-right from traditional fascism is their reliance on the postmodern themes of subversion and transgression. Nagle writes that the emergence of white nationalism does not signal a return of traditional conservative values, but are rather symbolic.

> "The absolute hegemony of the culture of nonconformism, self- expression, transgression, and irreverence for its own sake — an aesthetic that suits those who believe in nothing but the liberation of the individual and the id, whether they're on the left or the right. The principle- free idea of counterculture did not go away; it just became the style of the new right."

Nagle's emphasis on the distinctively transgressive nature of the alt-right is significant, as subversion is itself a defining feature of postmodernity. Flisfeder echoes this sentiment remarking that "now we are faced with a culture that champions subversion and transgression itself being transgressed by the so-called alt-right." Peterson's popular allure cannot be explained by his opportunistic use of Right-wing terminology alone, however. Capitalist realism also signifies the failure of the radical Left to posit an alternative to the sheer force of capitalism.

The Idea of Communism: A Horizon of an Alternative?

Not only does capitalist realism render the thinkability of an alternative to capital seem impossible, but one of the consequences of this very impossibility is that—like an open secret—the liberal discourse of identity politics has become a culturally dominant form of ideology. This discourse is an ideological cultural tendency, that is to say, it is not an organized social movement (much to the alt-right and Peterson's chagrin), but rather a discursive practice whereby social issues are characterized in the language of the seemingly irrefutable social unit: the individual. Since Hegel, we have known that every individual human being is also already a universal, that the "I is a We," that every time we utter the first-person singular "I" we simultaneously express the universal "I."

I am well aware that many on the Left will object to my use of the term "identity politics," as it is a heuristic rhetorical word used by the alt-right, and Peterson, to denounce those who they (mis)perceive to be on the radical far-Left. However, as Asad Haider notes in his book *Mistaken Identity*, identity politics has now become the ideological discourse of the neoliberal status quo, the same neoliberal establishment that is slowly losing its grip. Haider comments that identity politics has become so mainstream, in fact, that during her 2016 Presidential campaign, Hillary Clinton used "the language of 'intersectionality' and 'privilege' and used identity politics to combat the emergence of a left-wing challenge in the Democratic Party surrounding Bernie Sanders."

Peterson, of course, has made a name for himself for criticizing our ever-increasing politically correct culture. He blames the Humanities and the "postmodernist, cultural Marxists" for allegedly indoctrinating students with their ideology. Peterson himself admitted that he has found a way to exploit the moral outrage that is all-too predictable within the discourse of identity politics. His target is misplaced, but the fact that he has found an international audience is indicative of the current zeitgeist. As Žižek notes, Peterson "addresses what many of us feel goes wrong in the PC universe of obsessive regulation – the problem with him does not reside in his theories but in the partial truths that sustain them. If the left is not able to address these limitations of its own project, it is fighting a lost battle."

Curiously enough, radical left commentators and theorists have actually addressed the inherent limitations and contradictions of a political discourse that reduces all social injustices to individual identities, rather than social relations and collective solidarity. Haider reminds us that theorists such as Nancy Fraser, Adolph Reed Jr., Judith Butler, Wendy Brown, Alain Badiou (not to forget Žižek himself), and many others were, and continue to be, critical of the ideological tendency of identity politics. But being critical of identity politics from the standpoint of the far-Left is, unfortunately, not enough. The reason the discourse of identity politics has become the dominant ideological orientation for many activists and academics (and many opportunistic politicians) is because any alternative to capitalism as an economic and political order appears impossible. It is not a coincidence that identity politics is a discourse of reaction. That is to say, its reaction to all things politically incorrect is one of moral outrage and self-righteous indignation. The ideology of identity politics is also contradictory. The contradiction is that by soliciting the regulation of language and demanding more political correctness, this discourse ends up engendering its opposite. "In its contemporary ideological form," writes Haider, "identity politics is an individualist method. It is based on the individual's demand for recognition, and it takes that individual's identity as its starting point."

Essentially, the ideological parameters of identity politics are confined to the existing social institutions of contemporary capitalism. The point here is not to reduce all social antagonism to class struggle. Contrary to what some may believe, class is not an individuated identity, analogous to one's race, gender, sexual orientation, or ethnicity. Class is a social relation. This is not a plea for a class reductionism at the detriment of other social conflicts. But rather, as Haider, following Althusser, Jameson, and Žižek, social antagonisms are the ways in which capital consciously exploits and oppresses large segments of the population. Racism, for example, is just one of the ways through which capitalism exploits and oppresses. Class struggle overdetermines all other expressions of social antagonisms. Let me be absolutely clear: I am not implying or suggesting that the creation of the alt-right, or the recent popularity of far-Right nationalism is due to the prominence of identity politics. Identity politics is not responsible for the emergence of alt-right. Rather, the alt-right are dialectically related to one another insofar as they are both symptoms of capital. The 2008 financial crisis generated an economic and political event, and, as Flisfeder reminds us, there was a wave of Leftist protests (from Occupy Wall Street to the Arab Spring), none of these amounted to any radical change in capitalism. Unfortunately, in true Benjaminian fashion "the Left was incapable of producing change. There have been different material dimensions to each new rise of the Right in recent years, whether it is Trumpism, the Brexit vote, or the new alt- right. But in many ways, they are all reactionary responses to the failure of the Left in the wake of the crisis." The Left's failure to address the economic instability and the resurgence of financial crises is further complicated by the sordid history of the "Really Existing Communist" nations such as the Soviet Union, Mao's China, etc., in the 20th century.

Enzo Traverso begins his book *Left-Wing Melancholia* with a sobering and depressing diagnosis of our present historical moment. According to Traverso, what distinguishes the 21st century from the previous two centuries is the "eclipse of utopias." The 19th century began in the shadow of the French Revolution, "a rupture and a radical innovation," which "laid the basis for the birth of socialism, which developed with the growth of industrial society." Similarly, the 20th century was witness to the Russian Revolution, which "aroused a hope of emancipation that mobilized millions of men and women throughout the world." By stark contrast, however, our present century neither began in the wake of a monumental revolution, nor has it (yet) witnessed utopia in action. In the 21st century "historical time seems exhausted. The utopias of the past century have disappeared, leaving a present charged with memory but unable to project itself into the future. There is no visible 'horizon of expectation.'" Traverso remarks how in the last 200 years, our cultural imaginary was able to conceive of a better world, a progressive conception of humanity's future not only seemed possible, but it was in some way even inevitable. "Pushed forward by the French and Russian Revolution," writes Traverso, "the nineteenth and twentieth centuries projected themselves into a future identified with 'Progress' (industrial, technical, democratic, socialist). The twenty-first century, on the contrary, opens in a world without utopias, paralyzed by the historical defeats of communist revolutions."

Even though capitalist realism precludes, at least ostensibly, any possibility of thinking about an alternative to capitalism, Fisher did not resign himself to the sheer impossibility of a genuine alternative to global capital. He concludes *Capitalist Realism* with a reminder of the importance of seizing political opportunities to think of an alternative:

> "The long, dark night of the end of history has to be grasped as an enormous opportunity. The very oppressive pervasiveness of capitalist realism means that even glimmers of alternative political and economic possibilities can have

a disproportionately great effect. The tiniest event can tear a hole in the grey curtain of reaction which has marked the horizons of possibility under capitalist realism. From a situation in which nothing can happen, suddenly anything is possible again."

The horizon of possibility can, and has, opened up since the 2008 financial crisis. While capitalist realism has a firm grasp on our collective political imaginary, its clutch may be slipping. The U.K. Labour Party leader Jeremy Corbyn, a self-described democratic socialist who became leader in 2015, has managed to address the social and economic concerns in an unprecedented way. The Labour Party has, as of January 2018, over 500,000 registered members. In the United States, Bernie Sanders' 2016 Presidential campaign also managed to appeal to many who were negatively affected by the 2008 financial crisis and disillusioned with neoliberalism. More recently, the U.S. has seen democratic socialist candidates break into the mainstream with figures such as Alexandria Ocasio-Cortez. While the rising force of more Leftist politicians is certainly a welcome change from the Blairite and Clintonite neoliberalism, democratic socialism is encumbered by its own theoretical and practical limitations as it does not conceive of a social and economic society that can replace the capitalist political economy.

Jordan Peterson's international stardom—much like his fanbase—is symptomatic of the 2008 financial crisis and the myopia of capitalist realism. Rather than ridicule and mock Peterson's fanbase as being comprised of political reactionaries, racists, and sexists, it is essential for the radical Left to see the Peterson phenomenon as a general articulation of frustration of the Left's failures to not only address capitalism's economic crisis, but also to propose an alternative to capitalism.

Conclusion

Historically, the name for the alternative to capitalism was communism. Marx and Engels famously refer to communism as the abolition of bourgeois private property. "Let us finally imagine, for a change," writes Marx in *Capital*, "an association of free men, working with the means of production held in common." We in the 21st century have inherited the disastrous and tragic lived experience of 20th century communism—even if they were communist in name only. Even though capitalist realism has effectively made it nearly impossible to imagine a practical alternative to capital whereby the means of production are held in common, the Idea of communism remains paramount. As Alain Badiou notes "socialisms, which were the name of the communist Idea's only concrete forms, failed completely in the twentieth century." The horrific failures of the actualization of communism in the past century has paralyzed the Left to the extent that—to refer to Badiou's well-known formulation—contemporary radical Leftist politics combines the deconstruction of its past with the empty wait for its future. For Badiou, the cataclysmic failure of 20th century communism marks the end of a particular sequence of realizing the Idea of communism. In Badiou's language, an Idea that is "always the assertion that a new truth is historically possible." What Badiou calls the "communist hypothesis" is pertinent to any attempt at conceiving of an alternative to capitalism in the 21st century. In Badiou's own words, "we know that *communism is the right hypothesis*. Indeed, there is no other, or at least I am not aware of one. All those who abandon this hypothesis immediately resign themselves to the market economy, to parliamentary democracy—the form of state suited to capitalism—and to the inevitable and 'natural' character of the most monstrous inequalities." If communism is the correct hypothesis to a genuine alternative to the destructive and exploitative force of capitalism, then we need to seriously rethink its practical realization.

Indeed, as a young Marx wrote "as philosophy finds its material weapons in the proletariat, so the proletariat finds its spiritual weapons in philosophy [...] The *head* of this emancipation is *philosophy*, its *heart* the *proletariat*. Philosophy cannot be made a reality without the sublation [Aufhebung] of the proletariat, and the proletariat cannot be sublated itself without philosophy being made a reality." If we are to truly emancipate ourselves from capitalism and capitalist realism, we ought to muster up the courage to think that which seems impossible. Bertolt Brecht famously said that "because things are the way they are, things will not stay the way they are," and as the second decade of the 21st century draws to a close capitalism is certainly not staying the same. Our future remains indeterminate, it is up to us to ensure that the future is communist.

Popular videos include:

Žižek and the Double Blackmain

The Intellectual Dark Web is a Bad Sign

Can there be an Anti-SJW Left?

Answering Jordan Peterson on Marxism

Follow us on Facebook
at https://www.facebook.com/ZeroBooks and Twitter at https://twitter.com/Zer0Books

Bestsellers from Zer0 Books include:

Give Them An Argument
Logic for the Left
Ben Burgis
Many serious leftists have learned to distrust talk of logic. This is a serious mistake.
Paperback: 978-1-78904-210-8 ebook: 978-1-78904-211-5

Poor but Sexy
Culture Clashes in Europe East and West
Agata Pyzik
How the East stayed East and the West stayed West.
Paperback: 978-1-78099-394-2 ebook: 978-1-78099-395-9

An Anthropology of Nothing in Particular
Martin Demant Frederiksen
A journey into the social lives of meaninglessness.
Paperback: 978-1-78535-699-5 ebook: 978-1-78535-700-8

In the Dust of This Planet

Horror of Philosophy vol. 1

Eugene Thacker

In the first of a series of three books on the Horror of Philosophy, *In the Dust of This Planet* offers the genre of horror as a way of thinking about the unthinkable.

Paperback: 978-1-84694-676-9 ebook: 978-1-78099-010-1

The End of Oulipo?

An Attempt to Exhaust a Movement

Lauren Elkin, Veronica Esposito

Paperback: 978-1-78099-655-4 ebook: 978-1-78099-656-1

Capitalist Realism

Is There no Alternative?

Mark Fisher

An analysis of the ways in which capitalism has presented itself as the only realistic political-economic system.

Paperback: 978-1-84694-317-1 ebook: 978-1-78099-734-6

Rebel Rebel

Chris O'Leary

David Bowie: every single song. Everything you want to know, everything you didn't know.

Paperback: 978-1-78099-244-0 ebook: 978-1-78099-713-1

Kill All Normies

Angela Nagle

Online culture wars from 4chan and Tumblr to Trump.

Paperback: 978-1- 78535-543-1 ebook: 978-1-78535-544-8

Cartographies of the Absolute
Alberto Toscano, Jeff Kinkle
An aesthetics of the economy for the twenty-first century.
Paperback: 978-1-78099-275-4 ebook: 978-1-78279-973-3

Malign Velocities
Accelerationism and Capitalism
Benjamin Noys
Long listed for the Bread and Roses Prize 2015, *Malign Velocities* argues against the need for speed, tracking acceleration as the symptom of the ongoing crises of capitalism.
Paperback: 978-1-78279-300-7 ebook: 978-1-78279-299-4

Meat Market
Female Flesh under Capitalism
Laurie Penny
A feminist dissection of women's bodies as the fleshy fulcrum of capitalist cannibalism, whereby women are both consumers and consumed.
Paperback: 978-1-84694-521-2 ebook: 978-1-84694-782-7

Babbling Corpse
Vaporwave and the Commodification of Ghosts
Grafton Tanner
Paperback: 978-1-78279-759-3 ebook: 978-1-78279-760-9

New Work New Culture
Work we want and a culture that strengthens us
Frithjoff Bergmann
A serious alternative for mankind and the planet.
Paperback: 978-1-78904-064-7 ebook: 978-1-78904-065-4

Romeo and Juliet in Palestine

Teaching Under Occupation

Tom Sperlinger

Life in the West Bank, the nature of pedagogy and the role of a university under occupation.

Paperback: 978-1-78279-637-4 ebook: 978-1-78279-636-7

Ghosts of My Life

Writings on Depression, Hauntology and Lost Futures

Mark Fisher

Paperback: 978-1-78099-226-6 ebook: 978-1-78279-624-4

Sweetening the Pill

or How We Got Hooked on Hormonal Birth Control

Holly Grigg-Spall

Has contraception liberated or oppressed women? *Sweetening the Pill* breaks the silence on the dark side of hormonal contraception.

Paperback: 978-1-78099-607-3 ebook: 978-1-78099-608-0

Why Are We The Good Guys?

Reclaiming your Mind from the Delusions of Propaganda

David Cromwell

A provocative challenge to the standard ideology that Western power is a benevolent force in the world.

Paperback: 978-1-78099-365-2 ebook: 978-1-78099-366-9

The Writing on the Wall

On the Decomposition of Capitalism and its Critics

Anselm Jappe, Alastair Hemmens

A new approach to the meaning of social emancipation.

Paperback: 978-1-78535-581-3 ebook: 978-1-78535-582-0

Enjoying It

Candy Crush and Capitalism

Alfie Bown

A study of enjoyment and of the enjoyment of studying. Bown asks what enjoyment says about us and what we say about enjoyment, and why.

Paperback: 978-1-78535-155-6 ebook: 978-1-78535-156-3

Color, Facture, Art and Design

Iona Singh

This materialist definition of fine-art develops guidelines for architecture, design, cultural-studies and ultimately social change.

Paperback: 978-1-78099-629-5 ebook: 978-1-78099-630-1

Neglected or Misunderstood

The Radical Feminism of Shulamith Firestone

Victoria Margree

An interrogation of issues surrounding gender, biology, sexuality, work and technology, and the ways in which our imaginations continue to be in thrall to ideologies of maternity and the nuclear family.

Paperback: 978-1-78535-539-4 ebook: 978-1-78535-540-0

How to Dismantle the NHS in 10 Easy Steps (Second Edition)

Youssef El-Gingihy

The story of how your NHS was sold off and why you will have to buy private health insurance soon. A new expanded second edition with chapters on junior doctors' strikes and government blueprints for US-style healthcare.

Paperback: 978-1-78904-178-1 ebook: 978-1-78904-179-8

Digesting Recipes
The Art of Culinary Notation
Susannah Worth
A recipe is an instruction, the imperative tone of the expert, but this constraint can offer its own kind of potential. A recipe need not be a domestic trap but might instead offer escape – something to fantasise about or aspire to.
Paperback: 978-1-78279-860-6 ebook: 978-1-78279-859-0

Most titles are published in paperback and as an ebook. Paperbacks are available in traditional bookshops. Both print and ebook formats are available online.
Follow us on Facebook
at https://www.facebook.com/ZeroBooks
and Twitter at https://twitter.com/Zer0Books